In a Class by Himself

by Mike Peters

TOR®

A TOM DOHERTY ASSOCIATES BOOK
NEW YORK

This is a work of fiction. All the characters and events portrayed in this book are either products of the author's imagination or are used fictitiously.

GRIMMY™: IN A CLASS BY HIMSELF

http://www.grimmy.com

This book contains material previously published in a trade edition as *Grimmy: Friends Don't Let Friends Own Cats.*

A Tor Book
Published by Tom Doherty Associates, LLC
175 Fifth Avenue
New York, NY 10010

Tor Books on the World Wide Web:
http://www.tor.com

Tor® is a registered trademark of Tom Doherty Associates, LLC

ISBN: 0-812-57459-1

First edition: August 1996
First mass market edition: July 1999

Printed in the United States of America

0 9 8 7 6 5 4 3 2 1

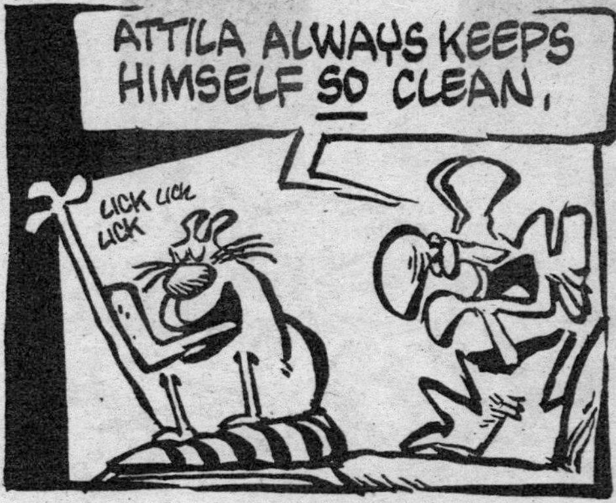
ATTILA ALWAYS KEEPS HIMSELF SO CLEAN.
LICK LICK LICK

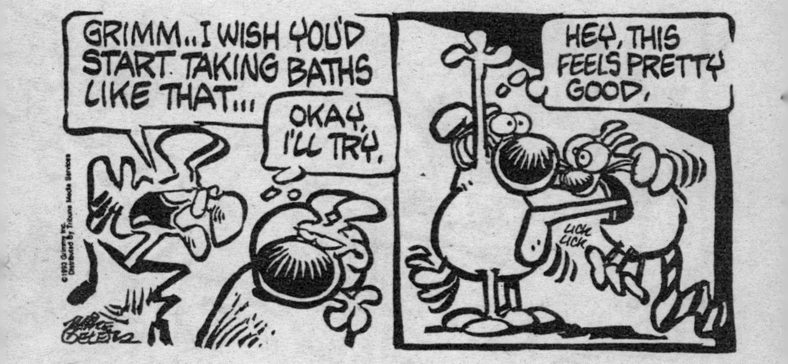
GRIMM..I WISH YOU'D START TAKING BATHS LIKE THAT...
OKAY, I'LL TRY.
HEY, THIS FEELS PRETTY GOOD.
LICK LICK
©1993 Grimmy Inc. Distributed By Tribune Media Services

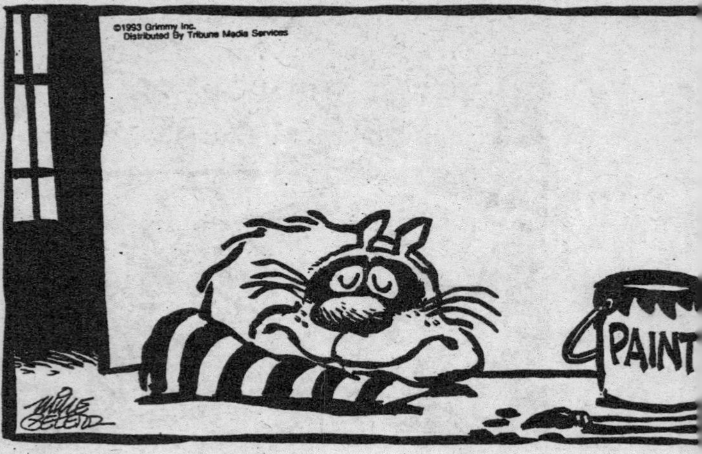
©1993 Grimmy Inc.
Distributed By Tribune Media Services
PAINT

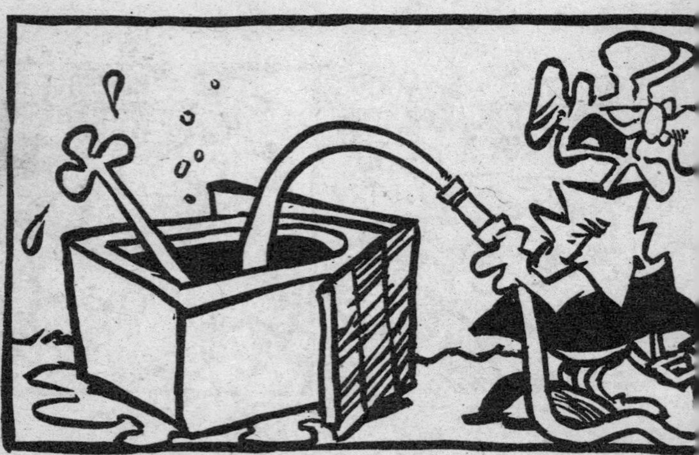

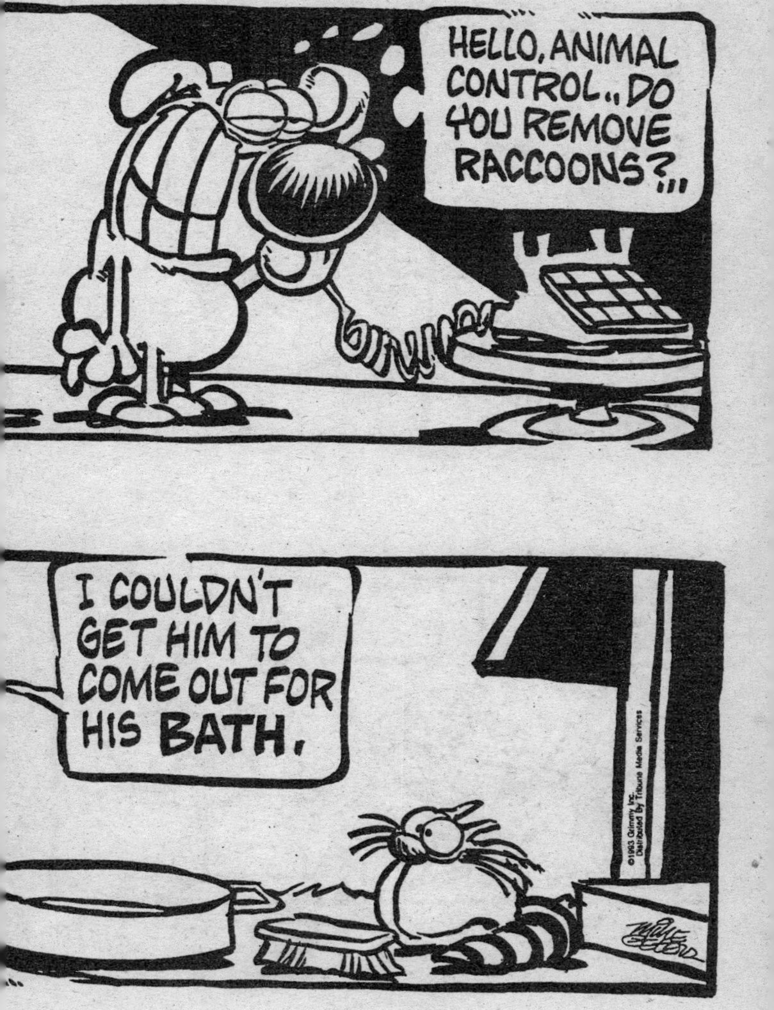
HELLO, ANIMAL CONTROL.. DO YOU REMOVE RACCOONS?...
I COULDN'T GET HIM TO COME OUT FOR HIS **BATH**.
©1983 Grimmy Inc. Distributed By Tribune Media Services

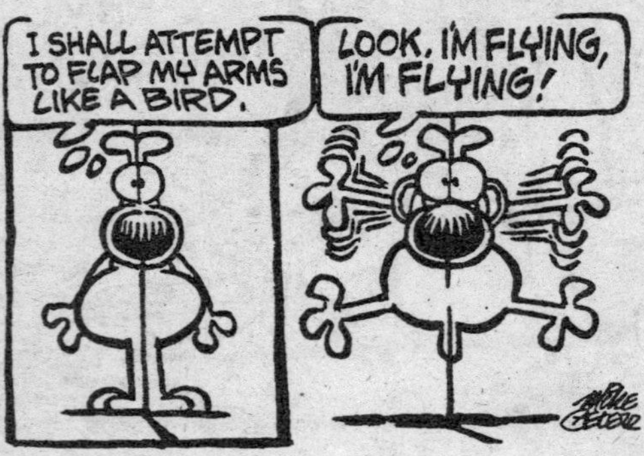
I SHALL ATTEMPT TO FLAP MY ARMS LIKE A BIRD.
LOOK, I'M FLYING, I'M FLYING!

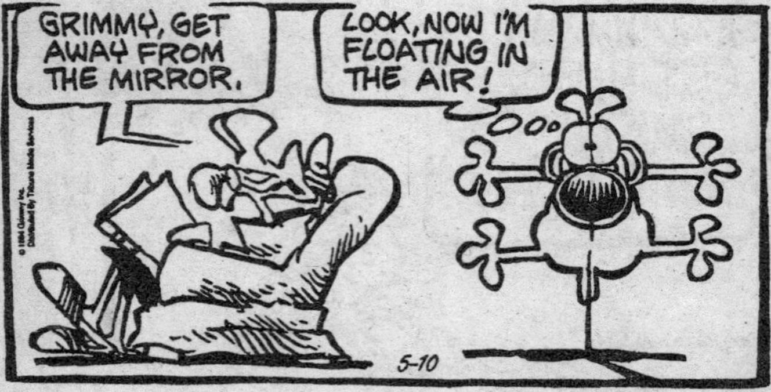
GRIMMY, GET AWAY FROM THE MIRROR.
LOOK, NOW I'M FLOATING IN THE AIR!
5-10

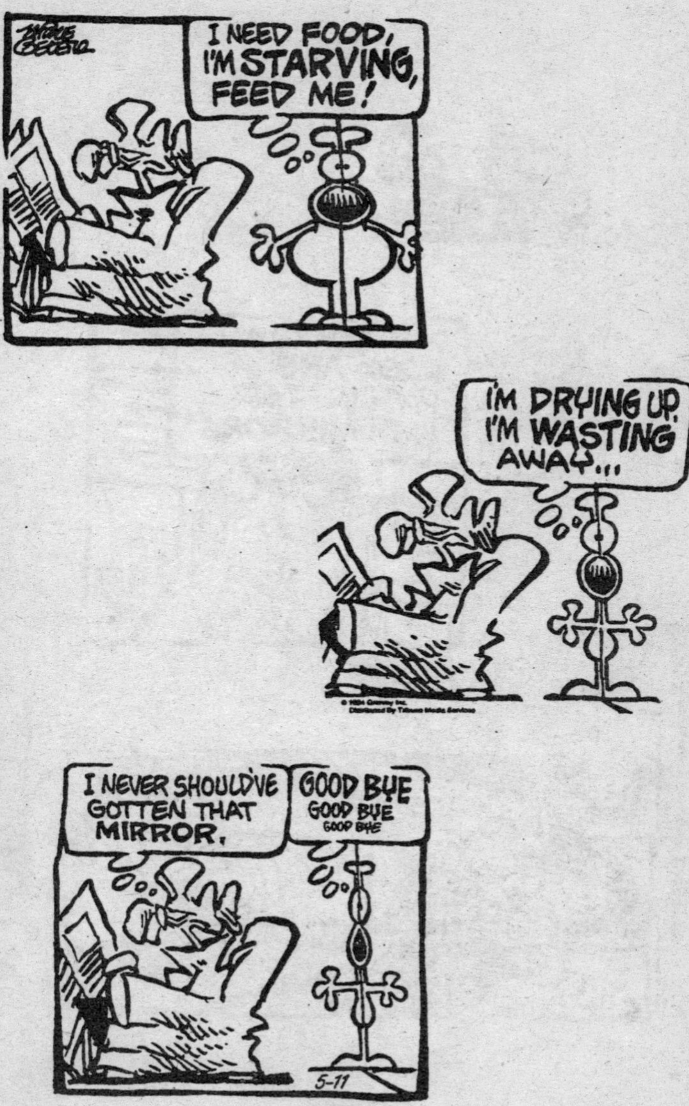

I NEED FOOD, I'M STARVING, FEED ME!
I'M DRYING UP, I'M WASTING AWAY...
I NEVER SHOULD'VE GOTTEN THAT MIRROR.
GOOD BYE GOOD BYE GOOD BYE
5-11

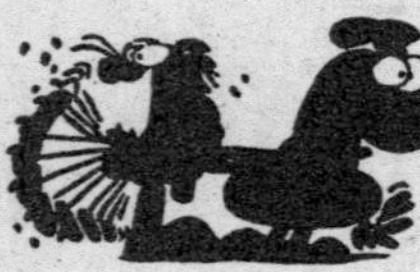

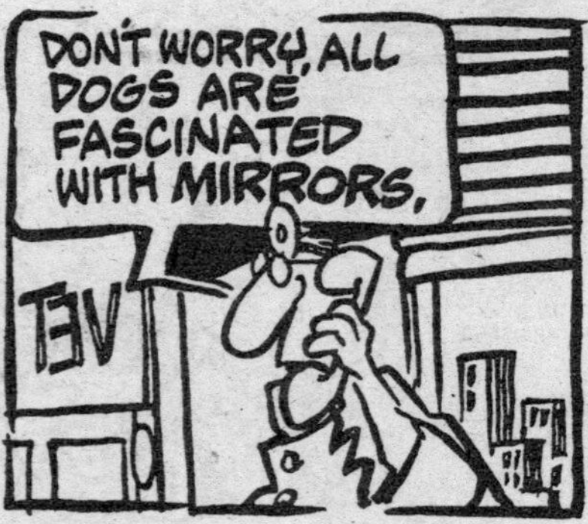
DON'T WORRY, ALL DOGS ARE FASCINATED WITH MIRRORS.

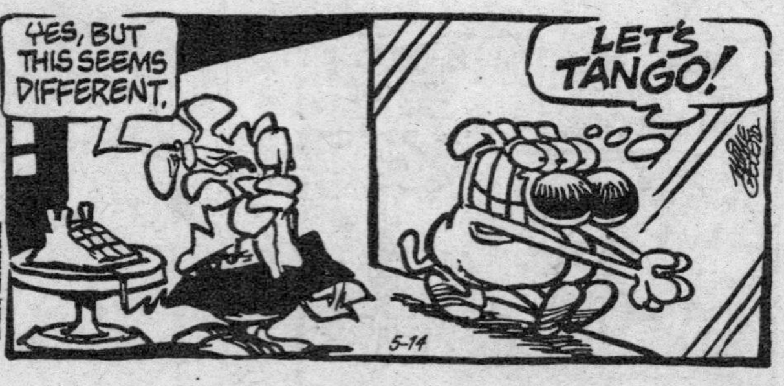
YES, BUT THIS SEEMS DIFFERENT.
LET'S TANGO!
5-14

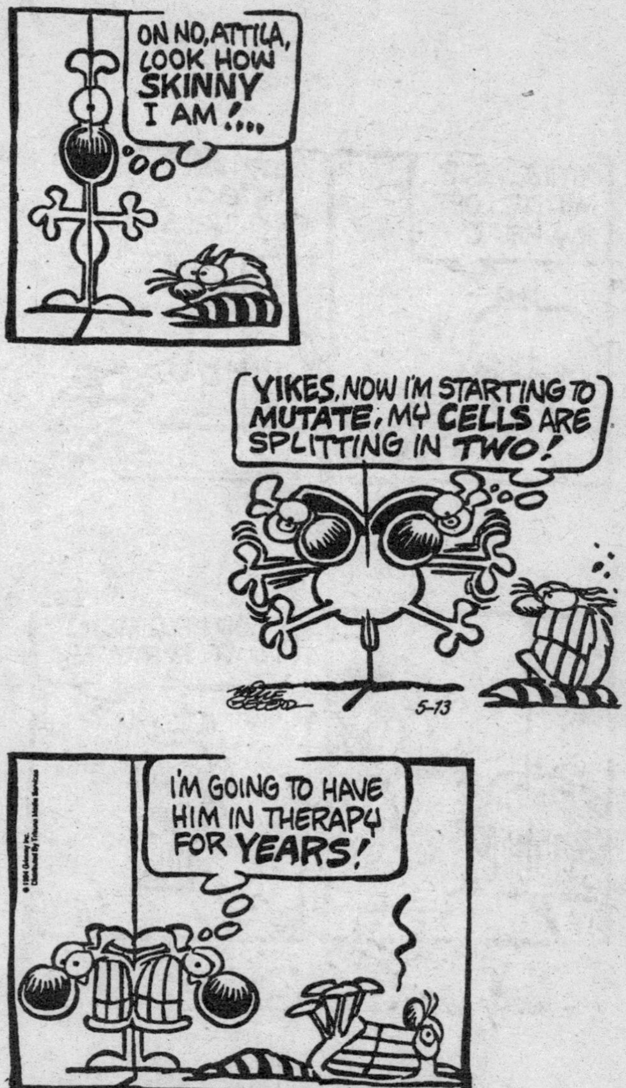
ON NO, ATTILA, LOOK HOW SKINNY I AM!....
YIKES, NOW I'M STARTING TO MUTATE, MY CELLS ARE SPLITTING IN TWO!
5-13
I'M GOING TO HAVE HIM IN THERAPY FOR YEARS!

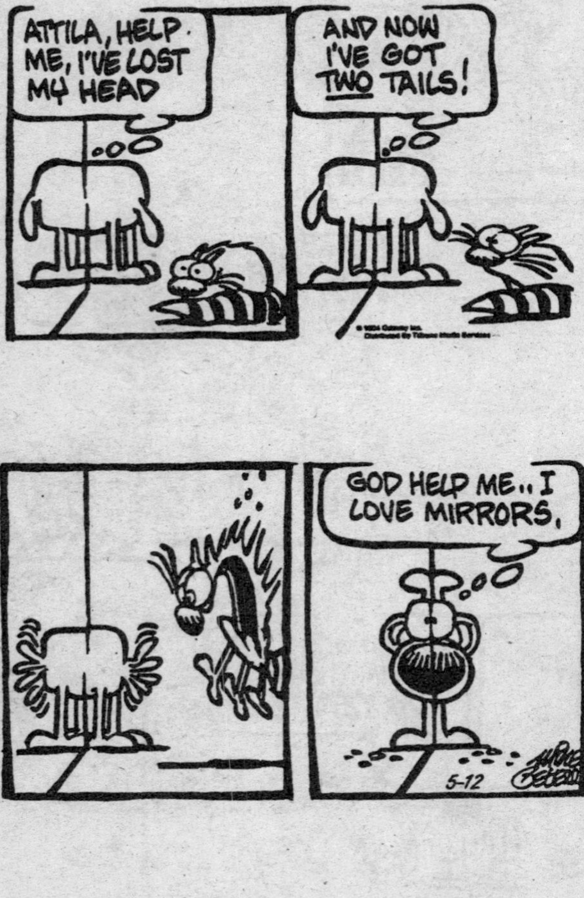
ATTILA, HELP. ME, I'VE LOST MY HEAD
AND NOW I'VE GOT TWO TAILS!
GOD HELP ME.. I LOVE MIRRORS,
5-12

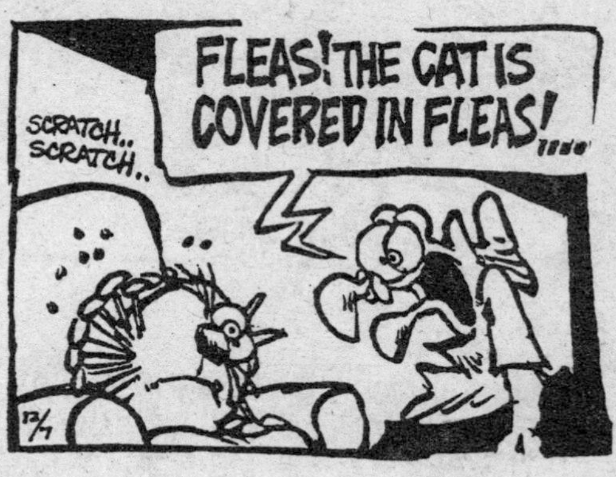
SCRATCH.. SCRATCH..
FLEAS! THE CAT IS COVERED IN FLEAS!

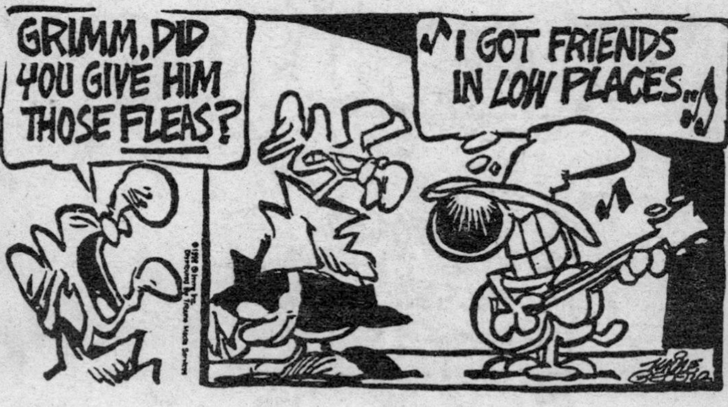
GRIMM, DID YOU GIVE HIM THOSE FLEAS?
I GOT FRIENDS IN LOW PLACES..

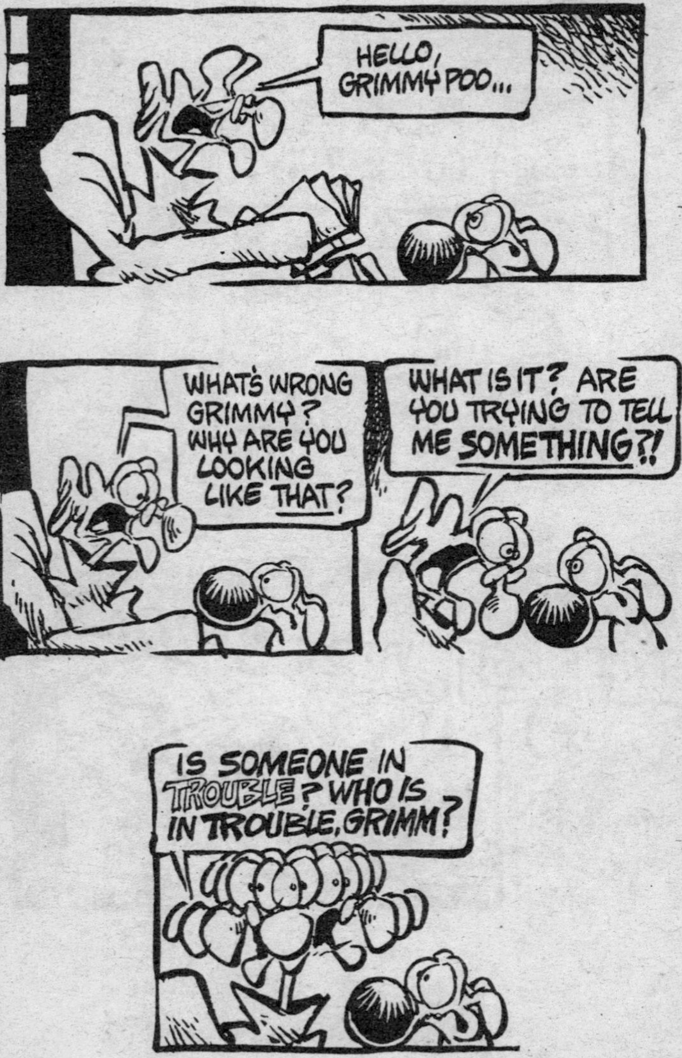
HELLO, GRIMMY POO...
WHAT'S WRONG GRIMMY? WHY ARE YOU LOOKING LIKE THAT?
WHAT IS IT? ARE YOU TRYING TO TELL ME SOMETHING?!
IS SOMEONE IN TROUBLE? WHO IS IN TROUBLE, GRIMM?

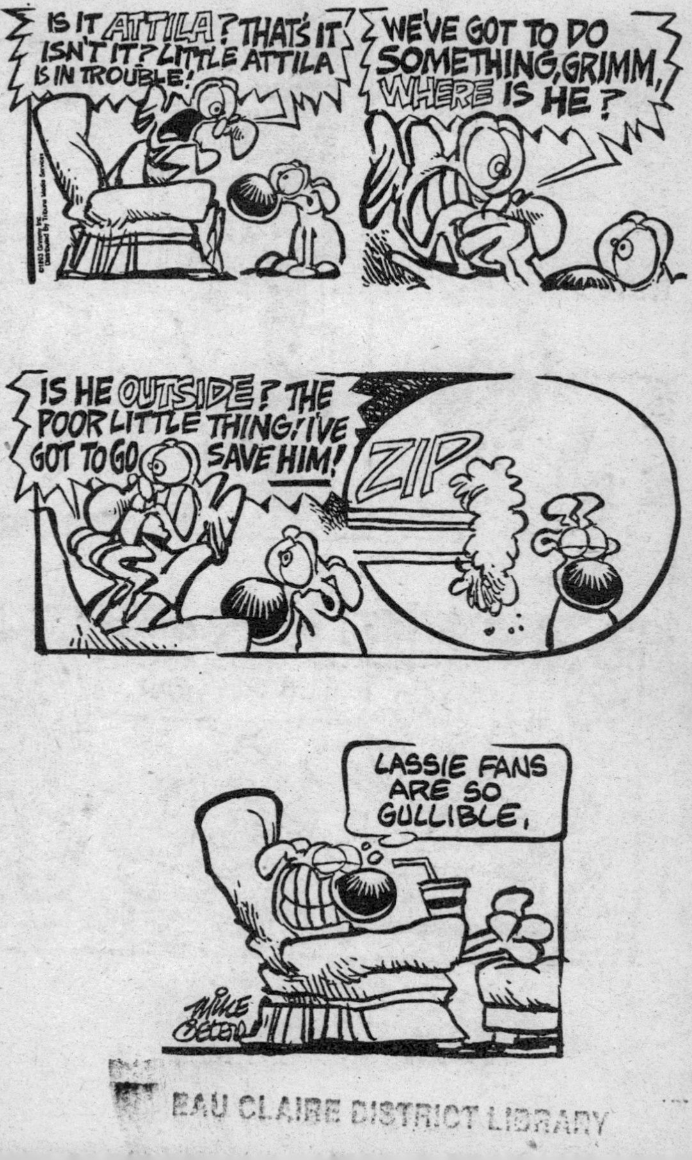
IS IT ATTILA? THAT'S IT ISN'T IT? LITTLE ATTILA IS IN TROUBLE!
WE'VE GOT TO DO SOMETHING, GRIMM, WHERE IS HE?
IS HE OUTSIDE? THE POOR LITTLE THING! I'VE GOT TO GO SAVE HIM!
ZIP
LASSIE FANS ARE SO GULLIBLE.

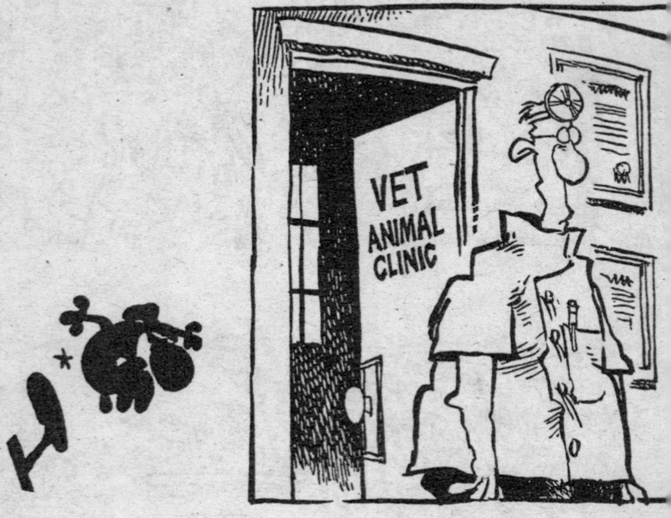
VET
ANIMAL
CLINIC

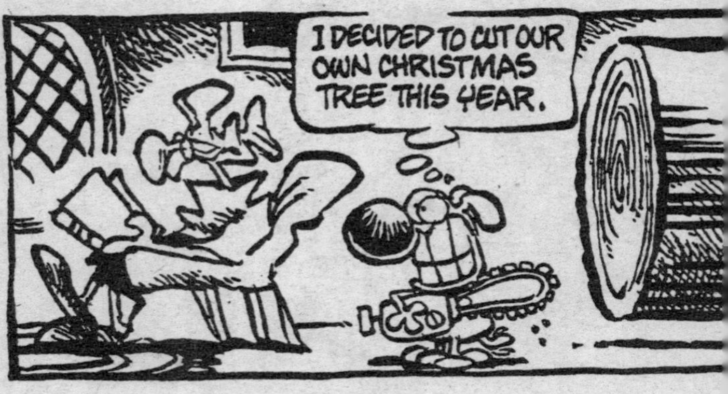
I DECIDED TO CUT OUR OWN CHRISTMAS TREE THIS YEAR.

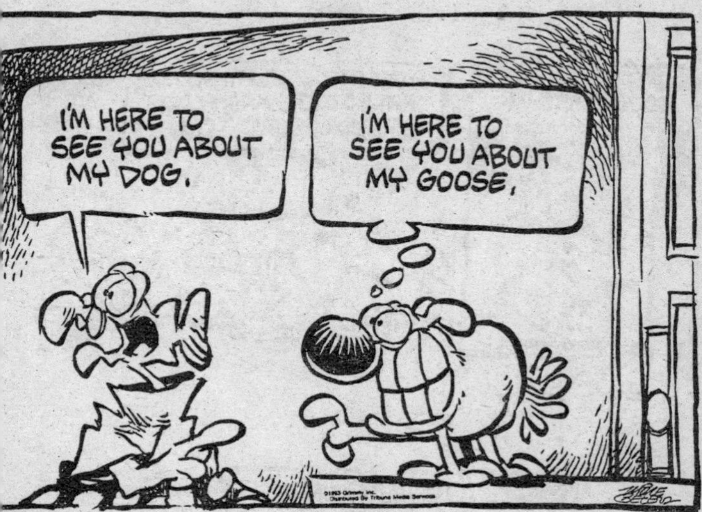
I'M HERE TO SEE YOU ABOUT MY DOG.
I'M HERE TO SEE YOU ABOUT MY GOOSE.

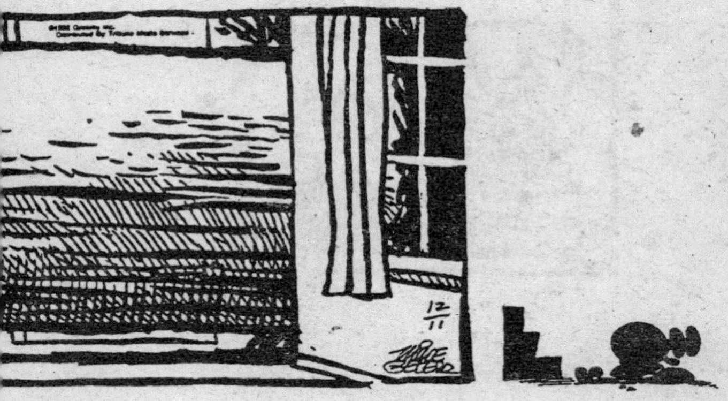
12/11

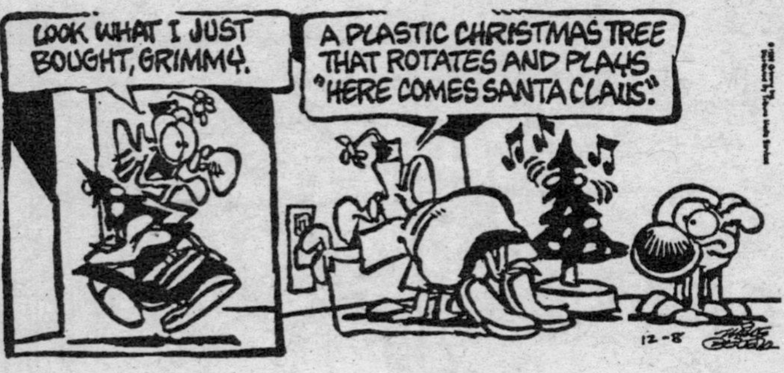
LOOK WHAT I JUST BOUGHT, GRIMMY.
A PLASTIC CHRISTMAS TREE THAT ROTATES AND PLAYS "HERE COMES SANTA CLAUS."
12-8

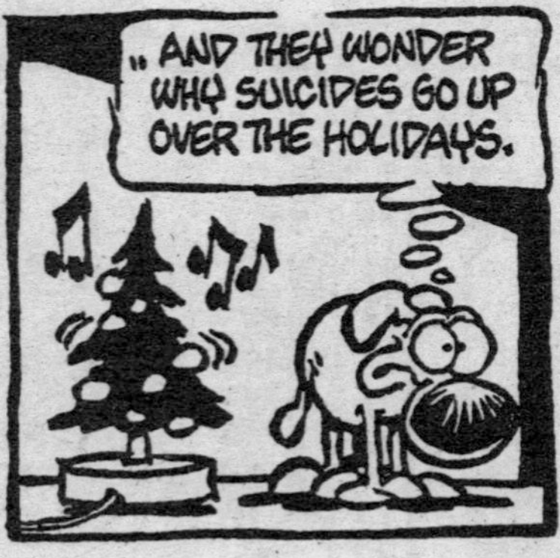
... AND THEY WONDER WHY SUICIDES GO UP OVER THE HOLIDAYS.

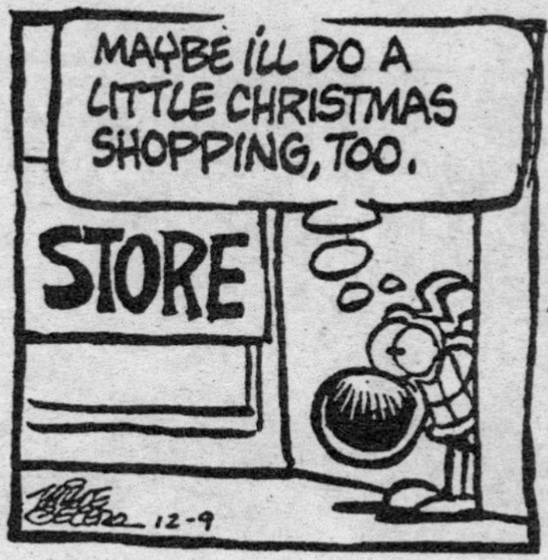
MAYBE I'LL DO A LITTLE CHRISTMAS SHOPPING, TOO.
STORE
12-9

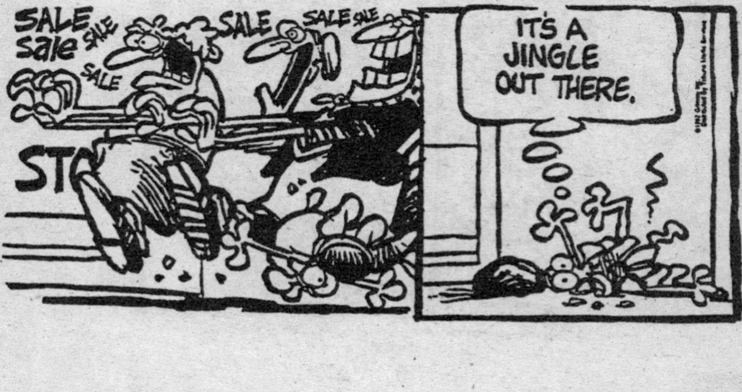
SALE
sale
SALE
SALE
SALE
SALE
SALE
ST
IT'S A JINGLE OUT THERE.

THIS CHRISTMAS, I'M SPRAYING PINE SCENT ON EVERYTHING.
SO ALL MY FURNITURE WILL SMELL LIKE FRESH PINE TREES.
!
YIP!!!
OOPS, WRONG THING TO SAY TO A DOG.
ZING
12-10

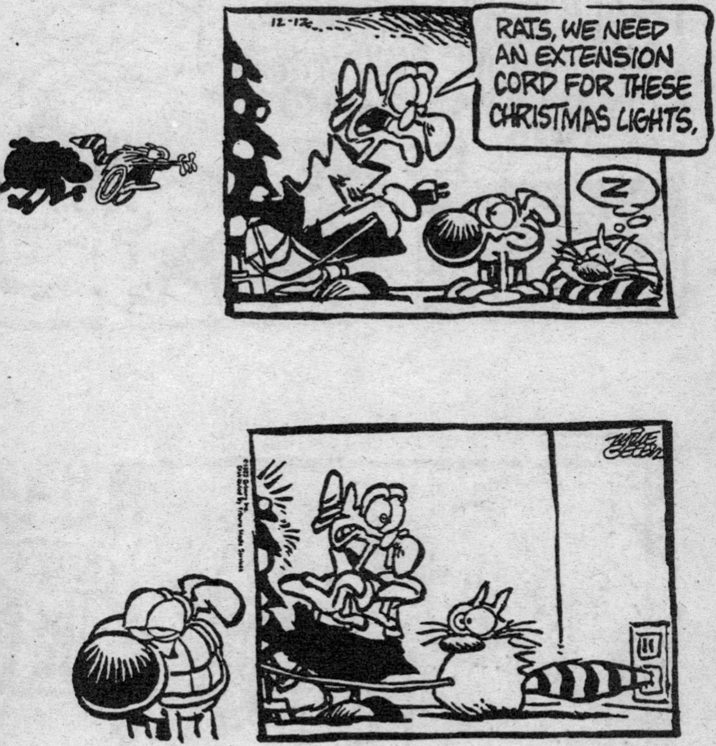
12-12
RATS, WE NEED AN EXTENSION CORD FOR THESE CHRISTMAS LIGHTS.
Z

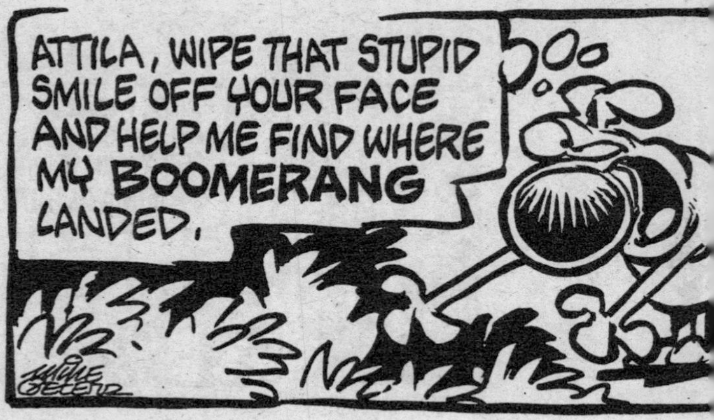
ATTILA, WIPE THAT STUPID SMILE OFF YOUR FACE AND HELP ME FIND WHERE MY BOOMERANG LANDED.

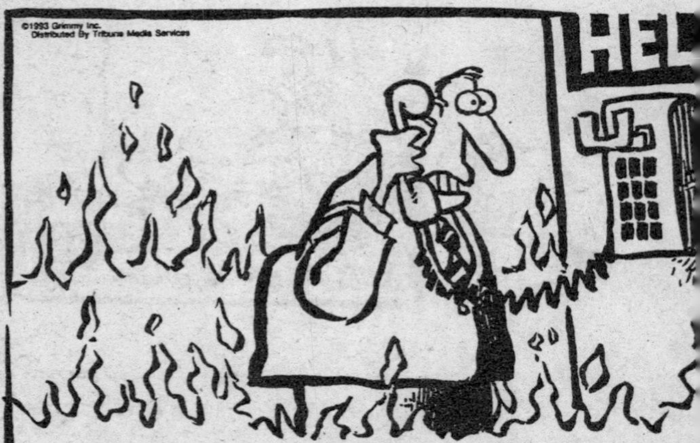
©1993 Grimmy Inc.
Distributed By Tribune Media Services

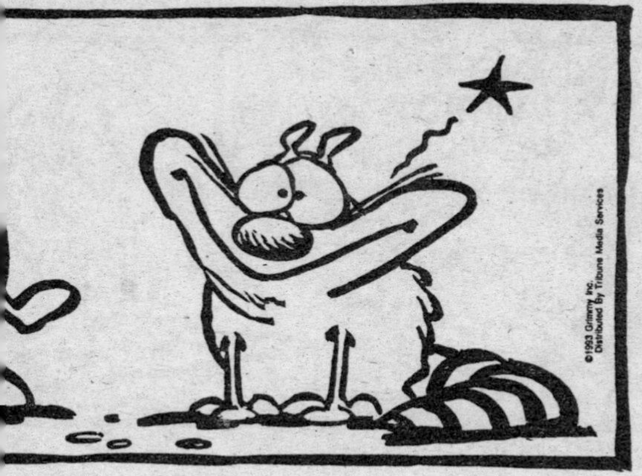
©1993 Grimmy Inc.
Distributed By Tribune Media Services

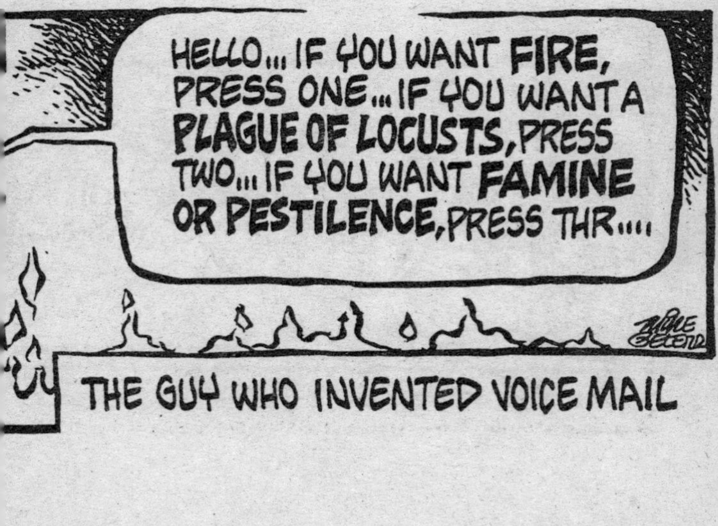
HELLO... IF YOU WANT FIRE, PRESS ONE... IF YOU WANT A PLAGUE OF LOCUSTS, PRESS TWO... IF YOU WANT FAMINE OR PESTILENCE, PRESS THR....
THE GUY WHO INVENTED VOICE MAIL

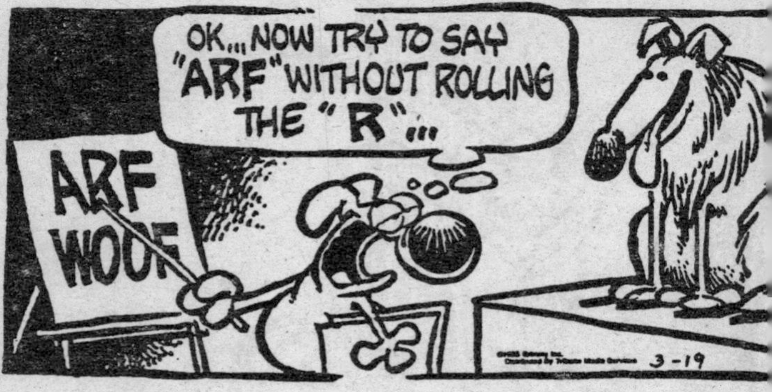
ARF
WOOF
OK... NOW TRY TO SAY "ARF" WITHOUT ROLLING THE "R"...
3-19

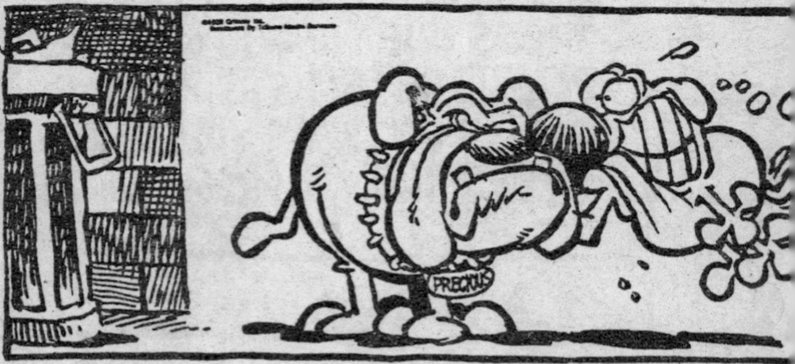
PRECIOUS

BEFORE LASSIE BECAME SUCCESSFUL, SHE HAD TO LOSE HER SCOTTISH ACCENT.

NO, ON SECOND THOUGHT, I THINK THAT THE NAME "PRECIOUS" IS VERY MACHO.

12-18

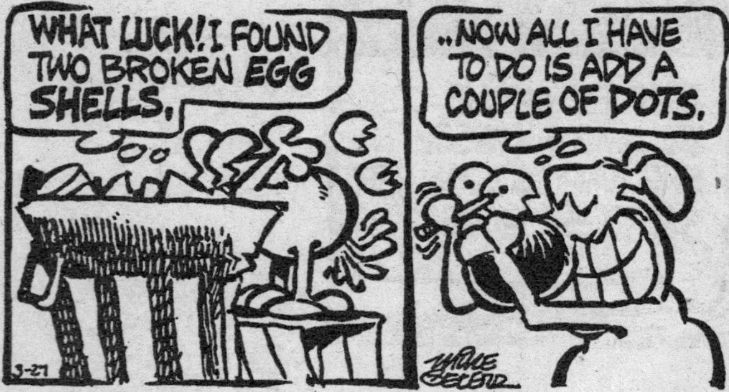
WHAT LUCK! I FOUND TWO BROKEN EGG SHELLS.
..NOW ALL I HAVE TO DO IS ADD A COUPLE OF DOTS.
3-27

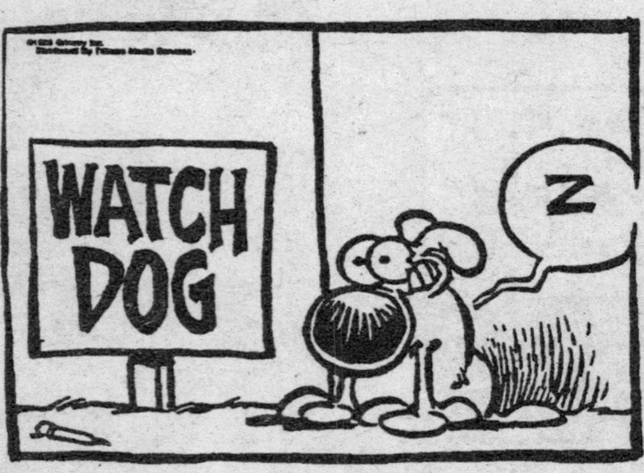
WATCH DOG
Z

GRIMMY, WHAT ARE YOU UP TO?
IT'S CHRISTMAS, I'M GOING TO THE NORTH POLE...
12-21

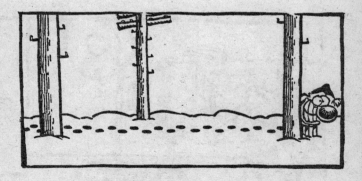

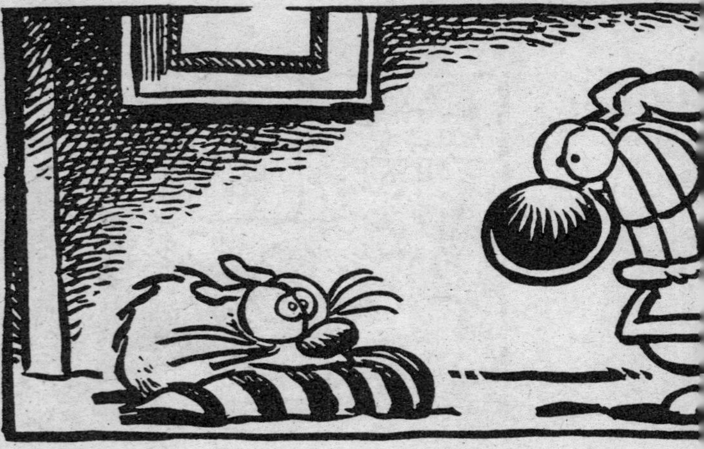

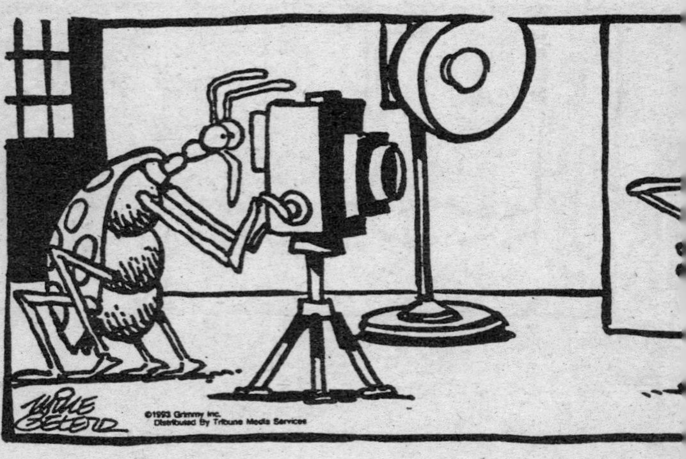
©1993 Grimmy Inc.
Distributed By Tribune Media Services

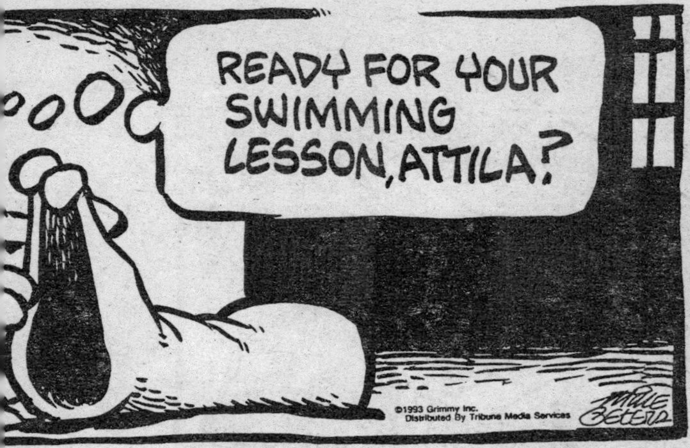
READY FOR YOUR SWIMMING LESSON, ATTILA?
©1993 Grimmy Inc.
Distributed By Tribune Media Services

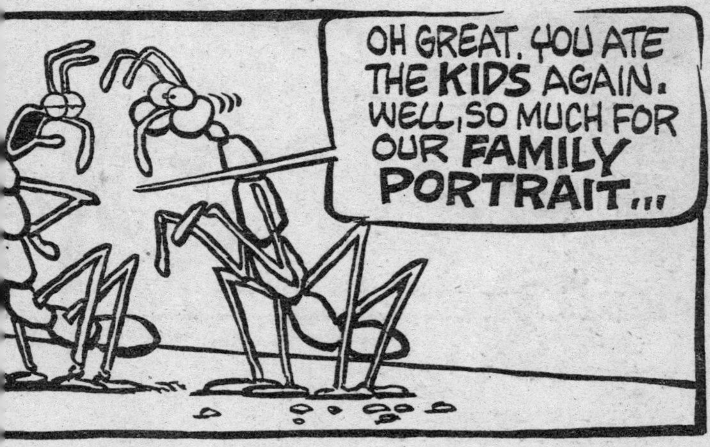
OH GREAT. YOU ATE THE **KIDS** AGAIN. WELL, SO MUCH FOR OUR **FAMILY PORTRAIT**...

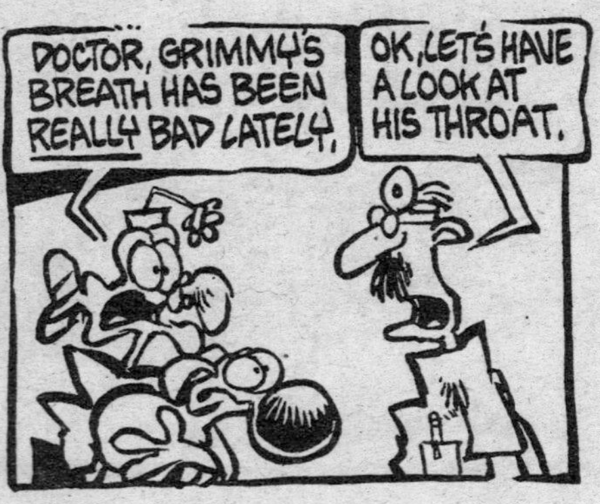
DOCTOR, GRIMMY'S BREATH HAS BEEN REALLY BAD LATELY.
OK, LET'S HAVE A LOOK AT HIS THROAT.

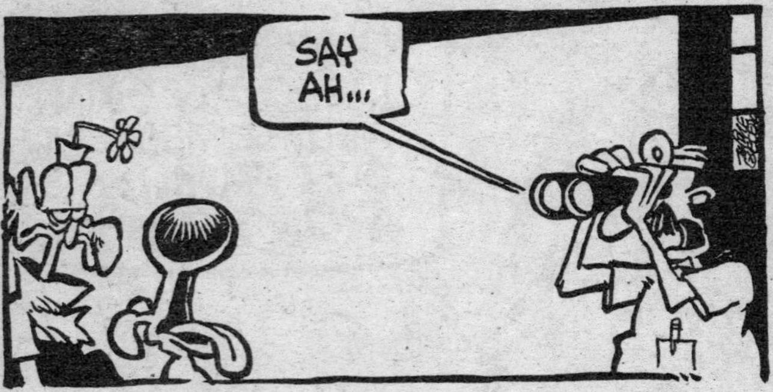
SAY AH...

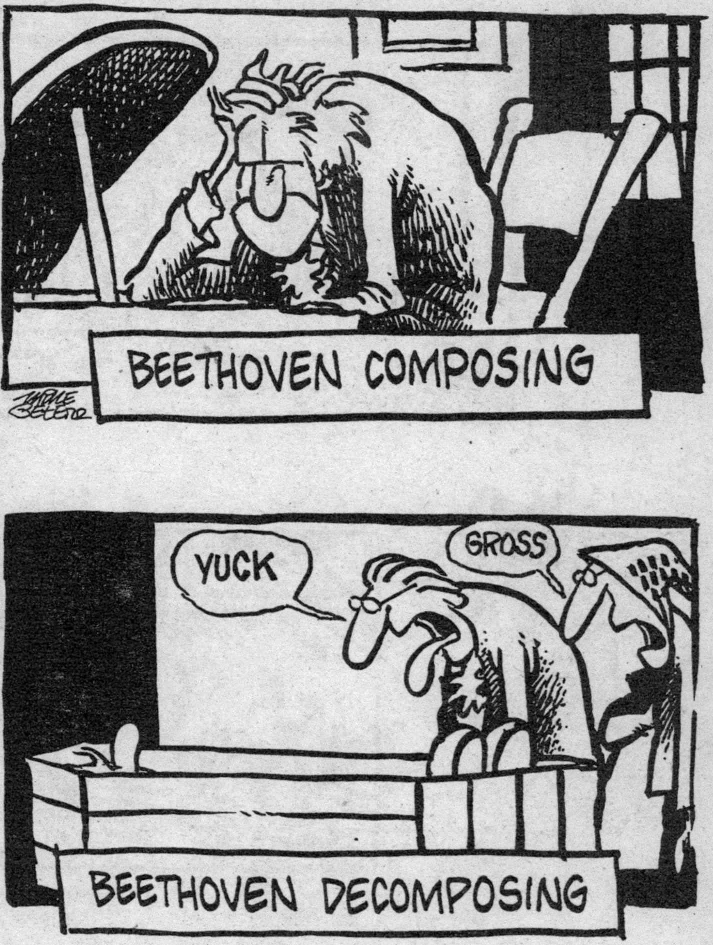
BEETHOVEN COMPOSING
YUCK
GROSS
BEETHOVEN DECOMPOSING

©1993 Grimmy, Inc.
Distributed By Tribune Media Services

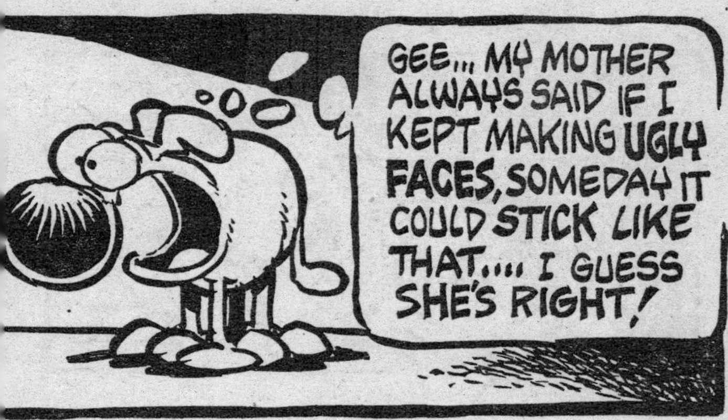
GEE... MY MOTHER ALWAYS SAID IF I KEPT MAKING UGLY FACES, SOMEDAY IT COULD STICK LIKE THAT.... I GUESS SHE'S RIGHT!

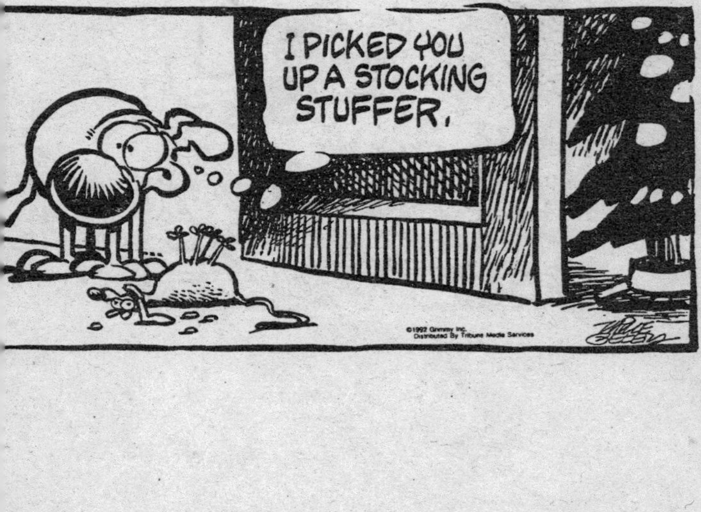
I PICKED YOU UP A STOCKING STUFFER.
©1992 Grimmy Inc.
Distributed By Tribune Media Services

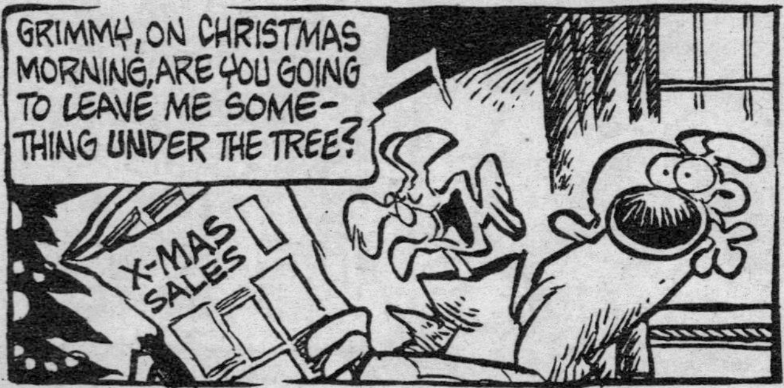
GRIMMY, ON CHRISTMAS MORNING, ARE YOU GOING TO LEAVE ME SOMETHING UNDER THE TREE?
X-MAS SALES

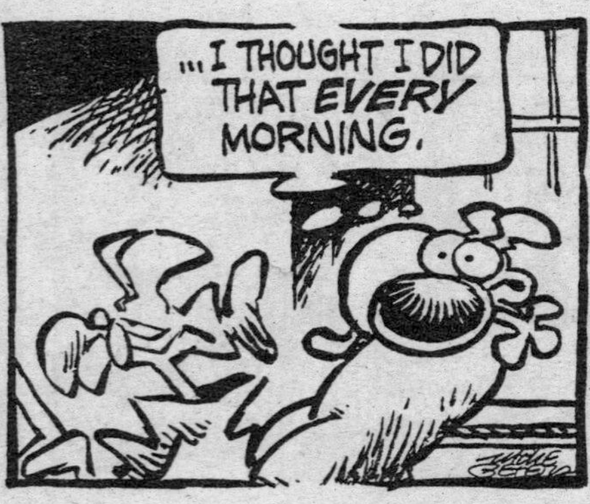
...I THOUGHT I DID THAT EVERY MORNING.

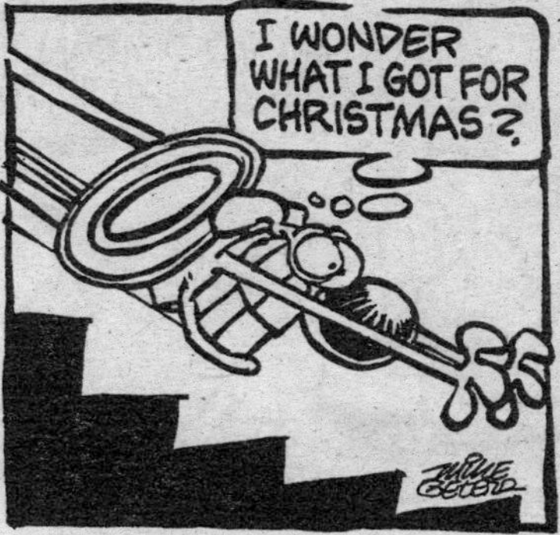
I WONDER WHAT I GOT FOR CHRISTMAS?

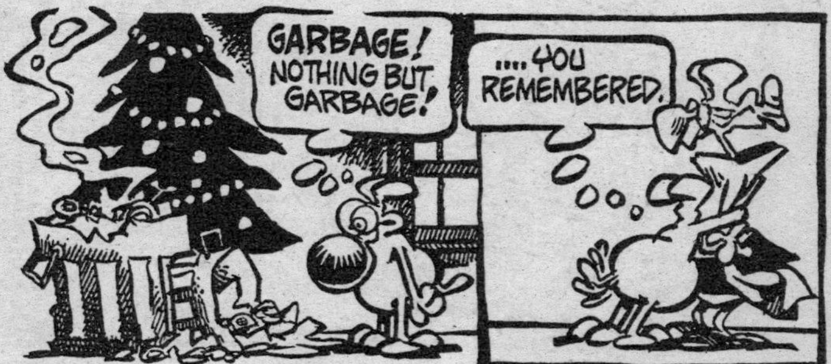
GARBAGE! NOTHING BUT GARBAGE!
....YOU REMEMBERED.

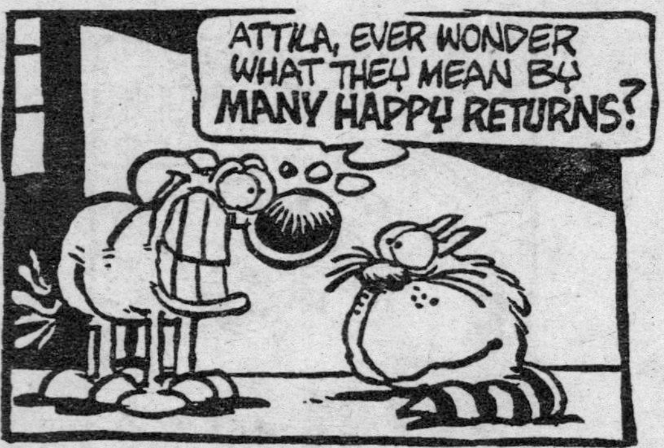
ATTILA, EVER WONDER WHAT THEY MEAN BY MANY HAPPY RETURNS?

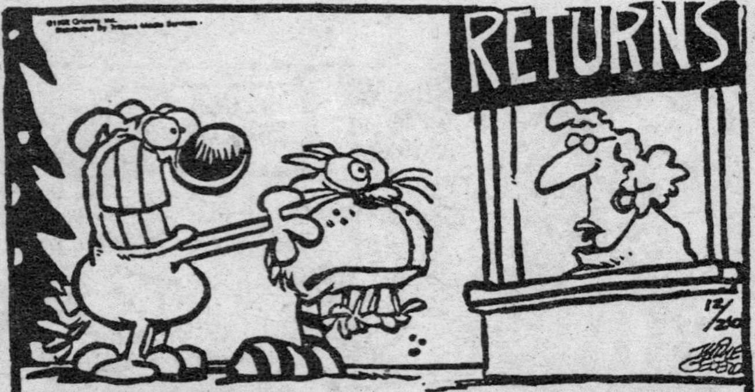
RETURNS

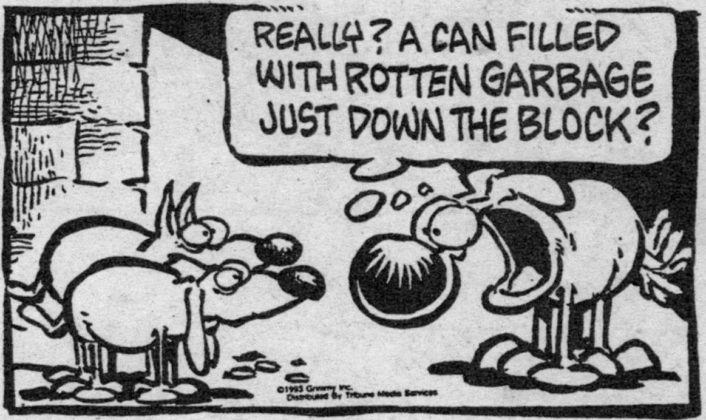
REALLY? A CAN FILLED WITH ROTTEN GARBAGE JUST DOWN THE BLOCK?
©1993 Grimmy Inc.
Distributed By Tribune Media Services

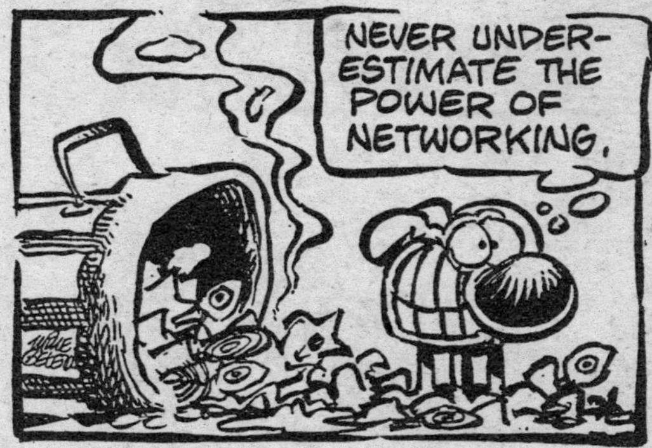
NEVER UNDER-ESTIMATE THE POWER OF NETWORKING.

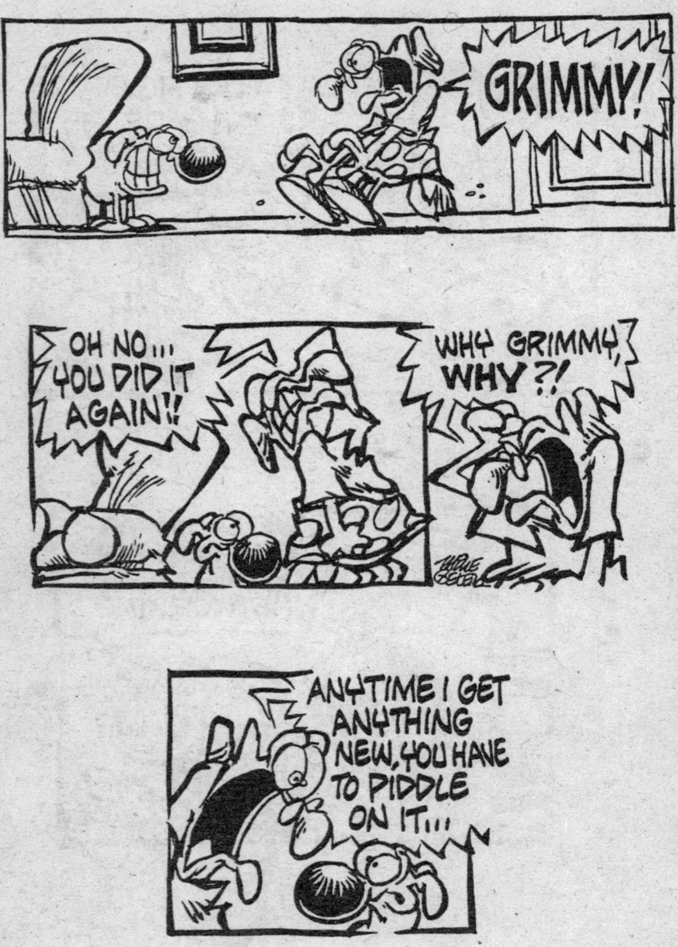
GRIMMY!
OH NO... YOU DID IT AGAIN!!
WHY GRIMMY, WHY?!
ANYTIME I GET ANYTHING NEW, YOU HAVE TO PIDDLE ON IT...

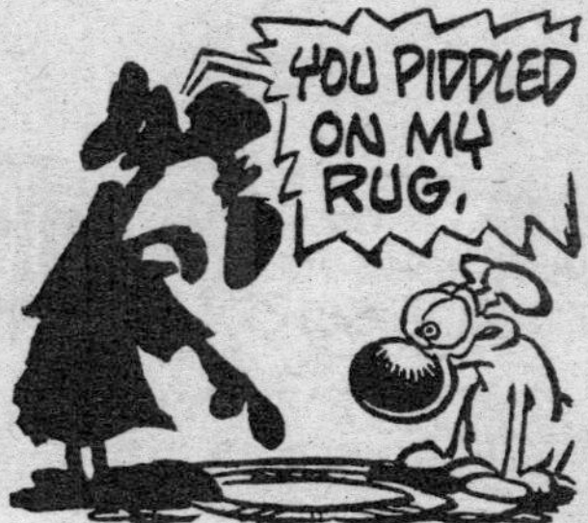
YOU PIDDLED ON MY RUG.

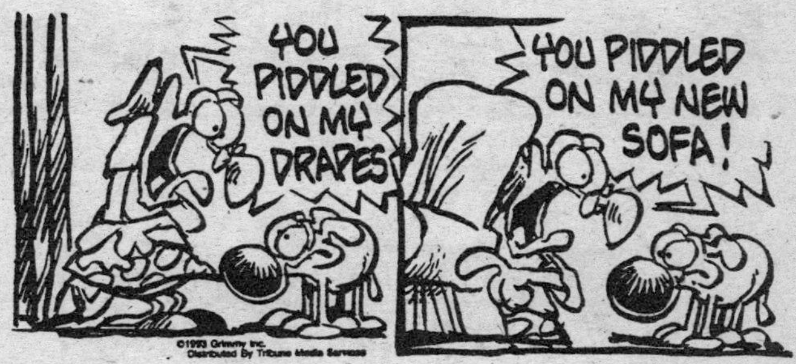
YOU PIDDLED ON MY DRAPES
YOU PIDDLED ON MY NEW SOFA!
©1993 Grimmy Inc.
Distributed By Tribune Media Services

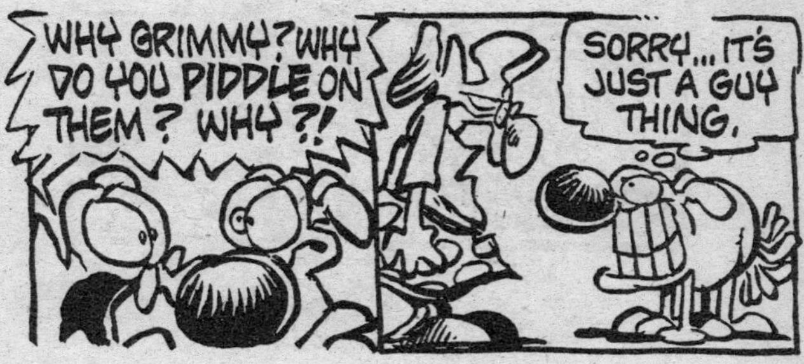
WHY GRIMMY? WHY DO YOU PIDDLE ON THEM? WHY?!
SORRY... IT'S JUST A GUY THING.

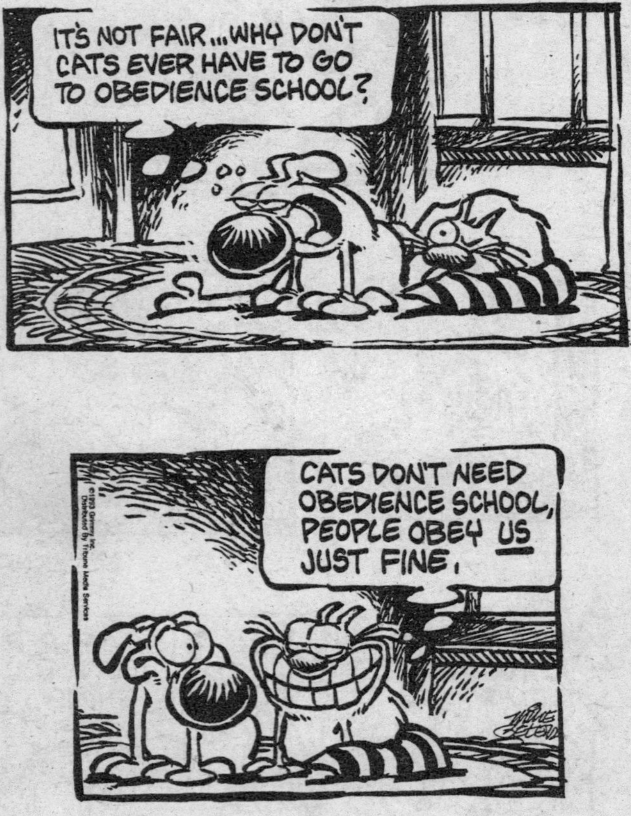
IT'S NOT FAIR... WHY DON'T CATS EVER HAVE TO GO TO OBEDIENCE SCHOOL?
CATS DON'T NEED OBEDIENCE SCHOOL, PEOPLE OBEY US JUST FINE.
©1993 Grimmy Inc. Distributed By Tribune Media Services

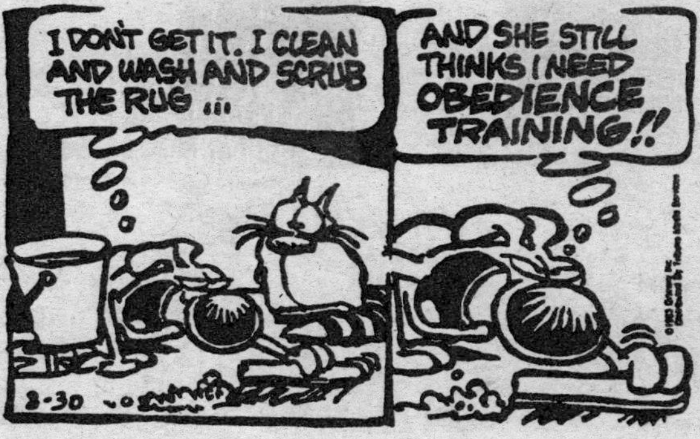
I DON'T GET IT. I CLEAN AND WASH AND SCRUB THE RUG ...
AND SHE STILL THINKS I NEED OBEDIENCE TRAINING!!
8-30

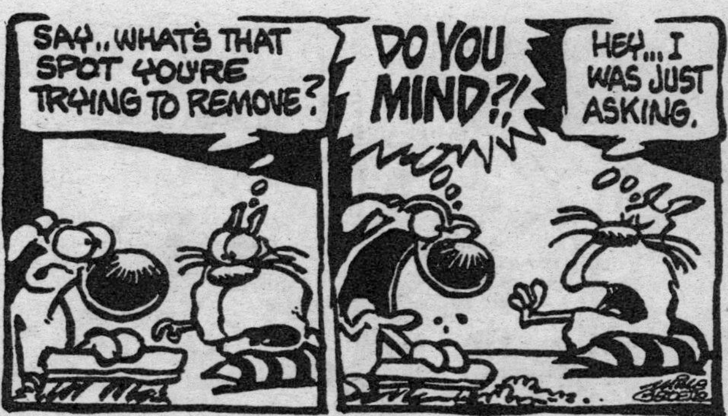
SAY.. WHAT'S THAT SPOT YOU'RE TRYING TO REMOVE?
DO YOU MIND?!
HEY... I WAS JUST ASKING.

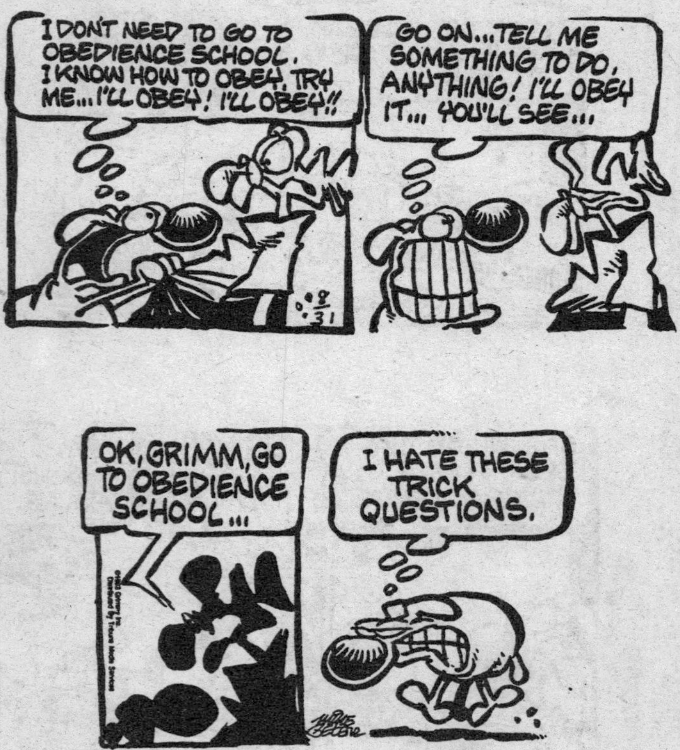
I DON'T NEED TO GO TO OBEDIENCE SCHOOL. I KNOW HOW TO OBEY. TRY ME... I'LL OBEY! I'LL OBEY!!
8/31
GO ON...TELL ME SOMETHING TO DO, ANYTHING! I'LL OBEY IT... YOU'LL SEE...
OK, GRIMM, GO TO OBEDIENCE SCHOOL...
I HATE THESE TRICK QUESTIONS.

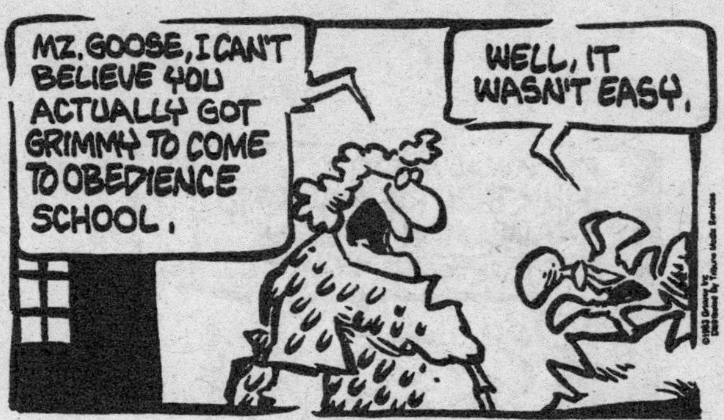
MZ. GOOSE, I CAN'T BELIEVE YOU ACTUALLY GOT GRIMMY TO COME TO OBEDIENCE SCHOOL.
WELL, IT WASN'T EASY.

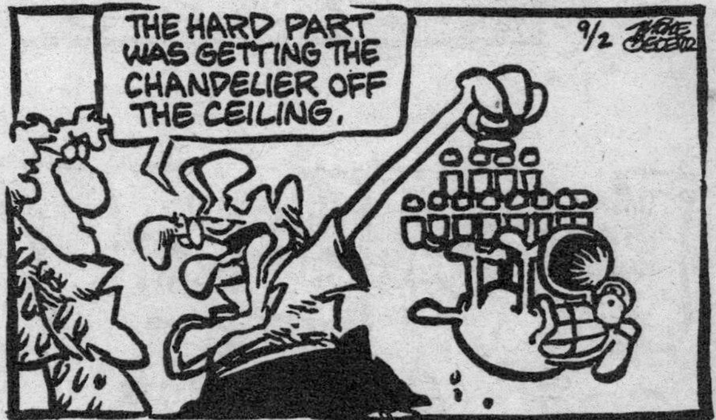
THE HARD PART WAS GETTING THE CHANDELIER OFF THE CEILING.
9/2

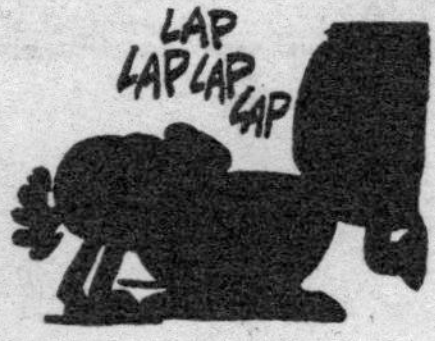
LAP LAP LAP LAP

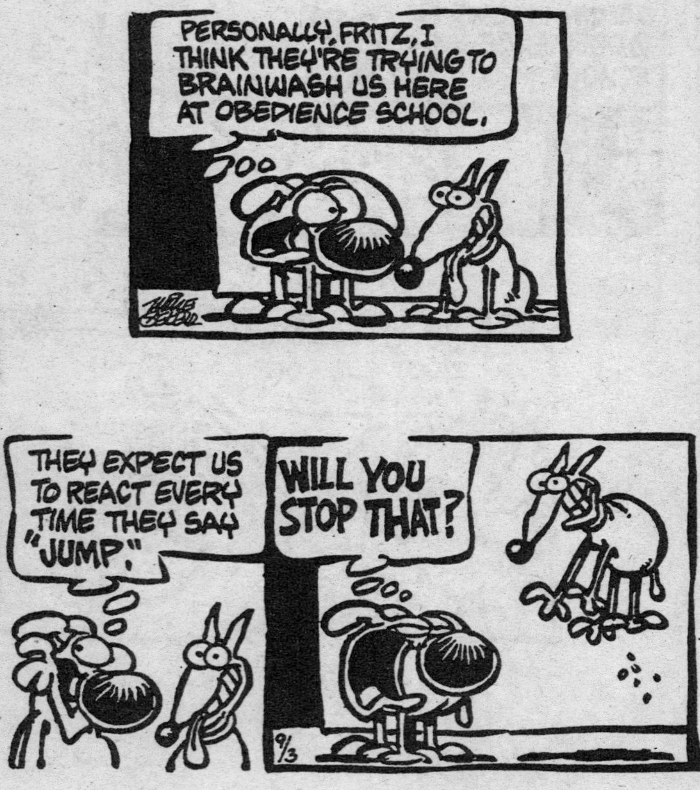
PERSONALLY, FRITZ, I THINK THEY'RE TRYING TO BRAINWASH US HERE AT OBEDIENCE SCHOOL.
THEY EXPECT US TO REACT EVERY TIME THEY SAY "JUMP."
WILL YOU STOP THAT?
9/3

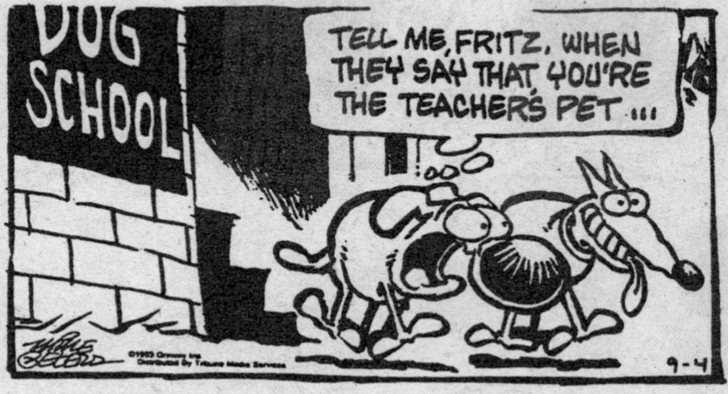
DOG SCHOOL
TELL ME, FRITZ, WHEN THEY SAY THAT YOU'RE THE TEACHER'S PET ...
9-4

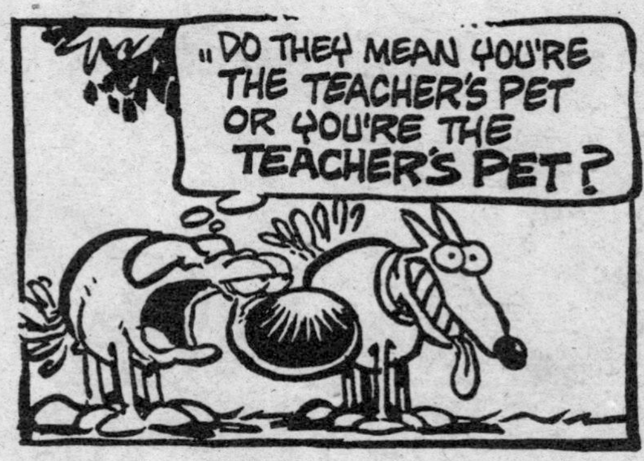
... DO THEY MEAN YOU'RE THE TEACHER'S PET OR YOU'RE THE TEACHER'S PET?

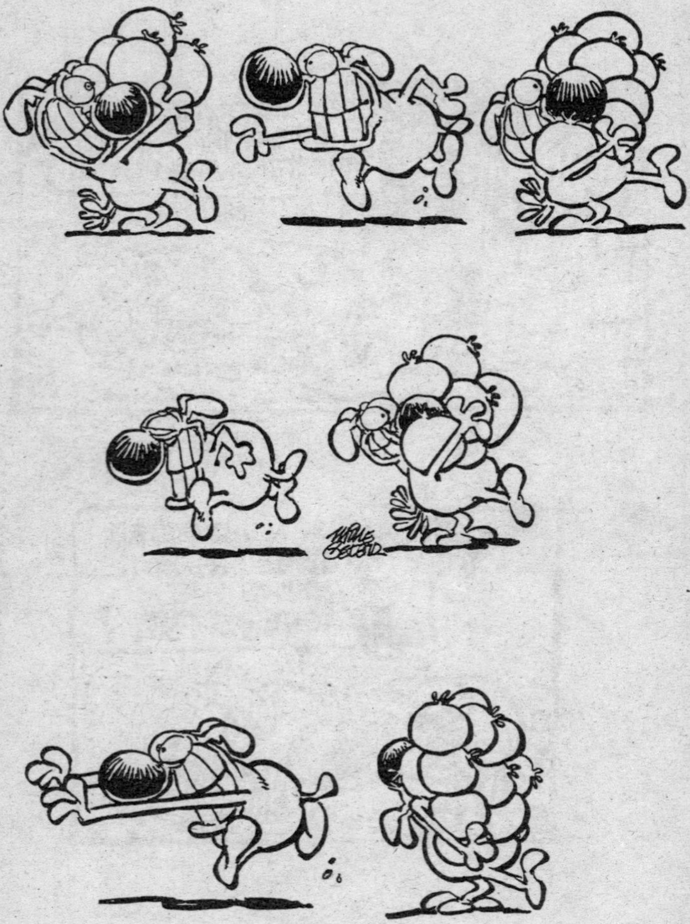

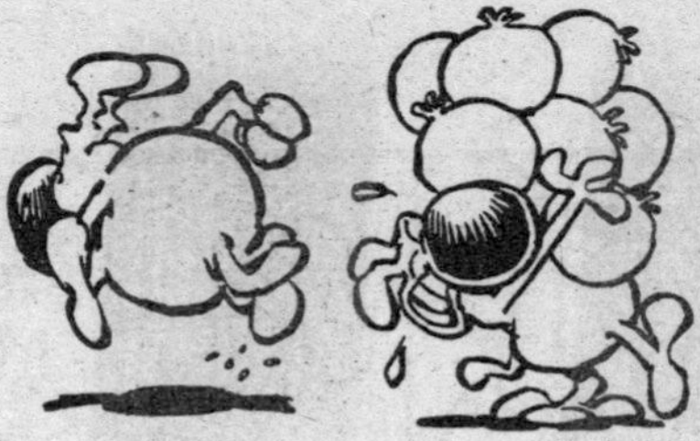

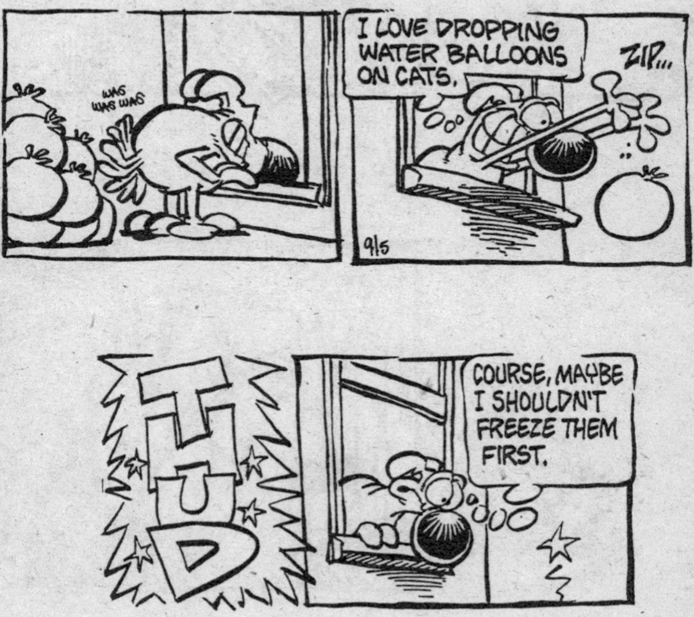
WAS WAS WAS
I LOVE DROPPING WATER BALLOONS ON CATS.
ZIP...
9/5
TUD
COURSE, MAYBE I SHOULDN'T FREEZE THEM FIRST.

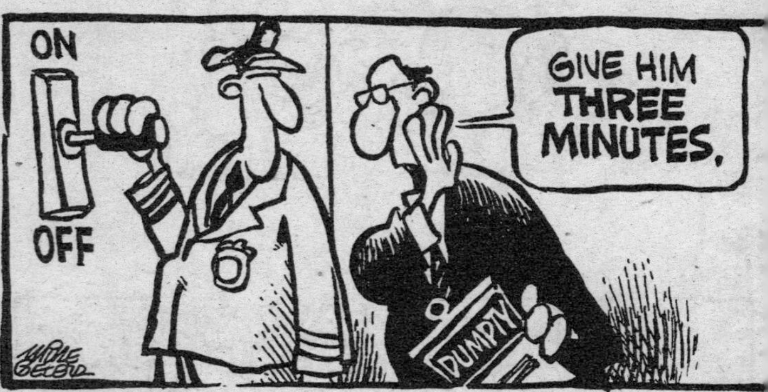
ON
OFF
GIVE HIM THREE MINUTES.
DUMPTY

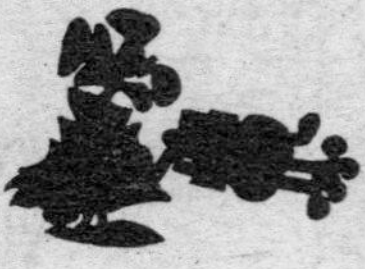

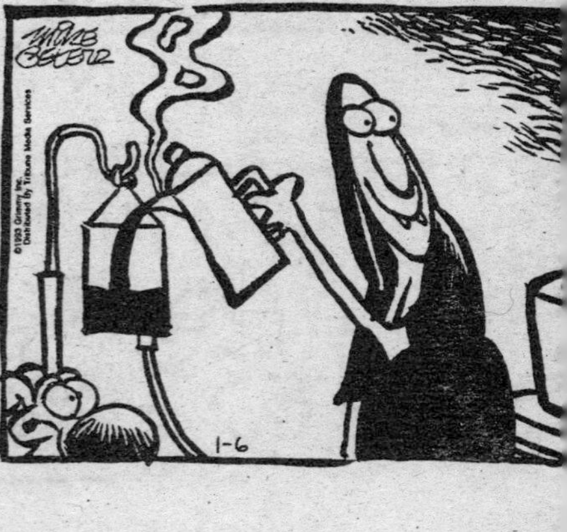
©1993 Grimmy Inc.
Distributed by Tribune Media Services
1-6

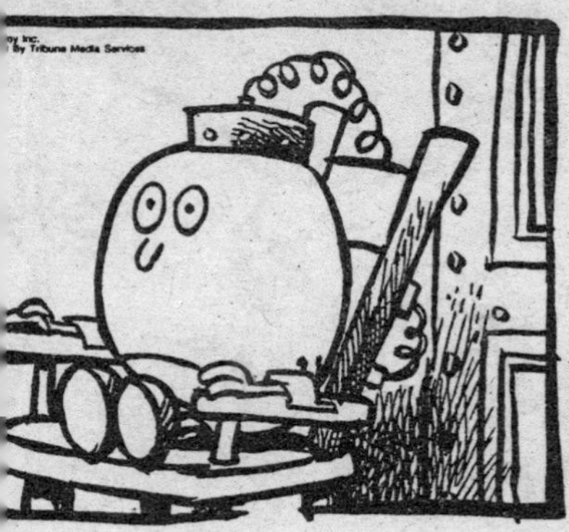
by Tribune Media Services

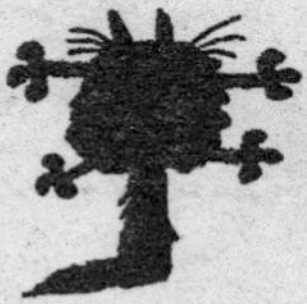

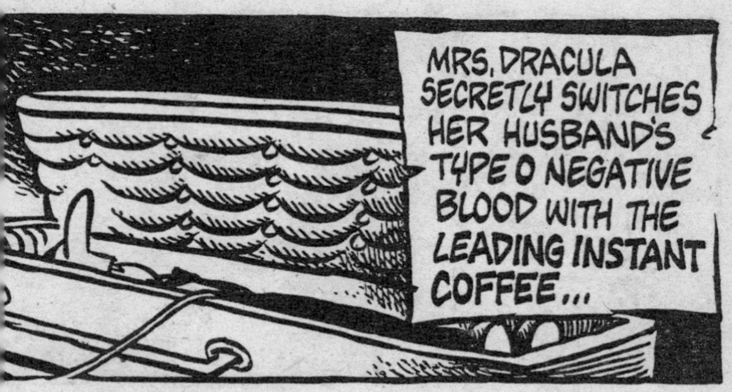
MRS. DRACULA SECRETLY SWITCHES HER HUSBAND'S TYPE O NEGATIVE BLOOD WITH THE LEADING INSTANT COFFEE...

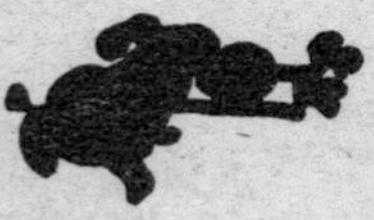

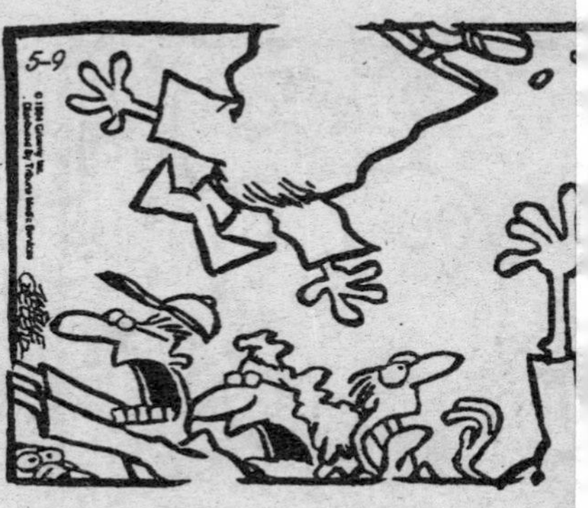
5-9

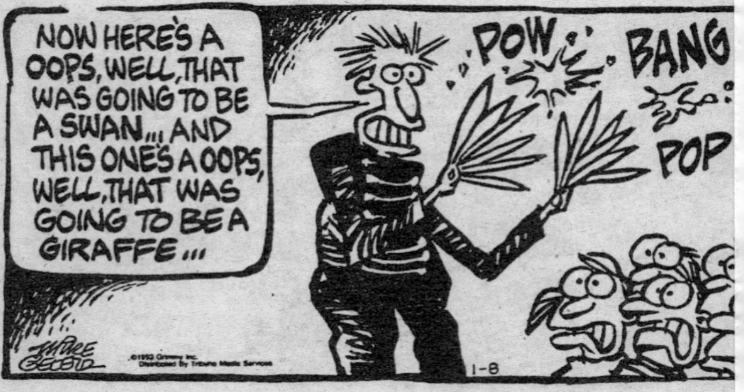
NOW HERE'S A OOPS, WELL, THAT WAS GOING TO BE A SWAN... AND THIS ONE'S A OOPS, WELL, THAT WAS GOING TO BE A GIRAFFE...
POW
BANG
POP
©1993 Grimmy Inc. Distributed By Tribune Media Services
1-8

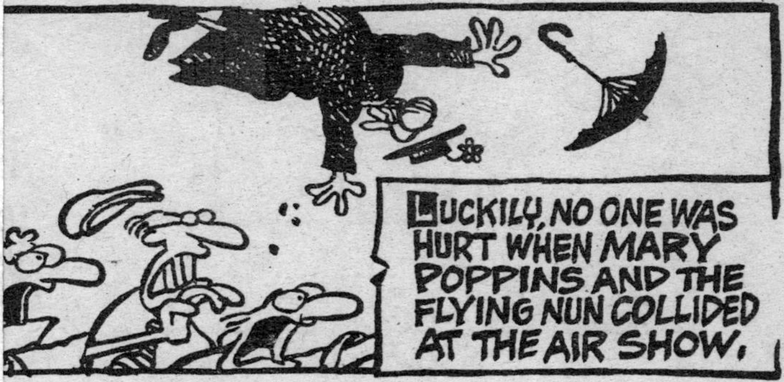
LUCKILY, NO ONE WAS HURT WHEN MARY POPPINS AND THE FLYING NUN COLLIDED AT THE AIR SHOW.

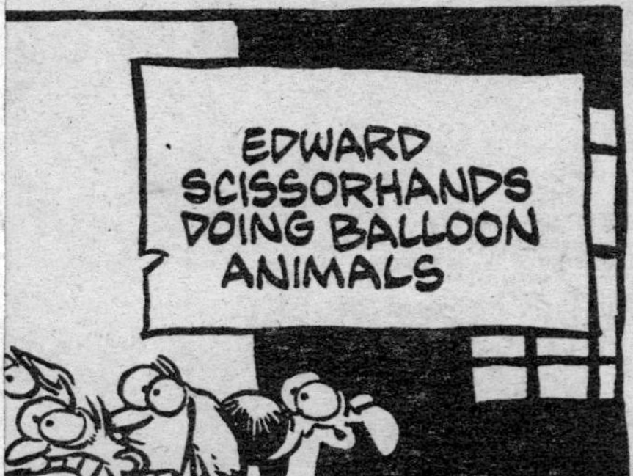
EDWARD SCISSORHANDS DOING BALLOON ANIMALS

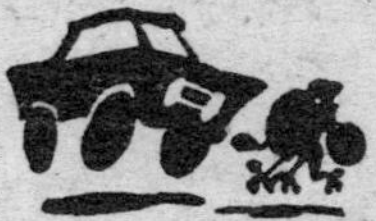

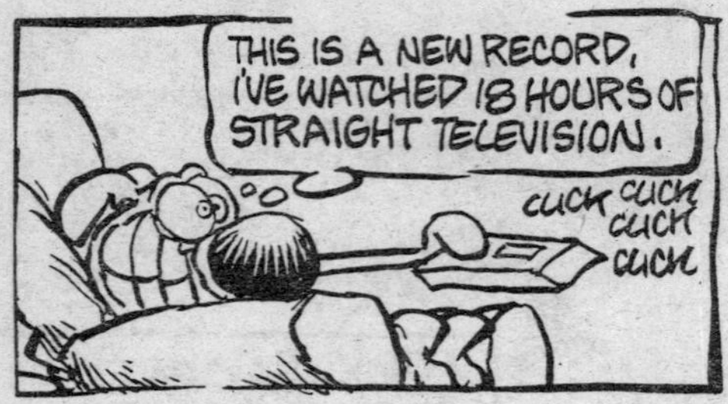
THIS IS A NEW RECORD, I'VE WATCHED 18 HOURS OF STRAIGHT TELEVISION.
CLICK CLICK CLICK CLICK

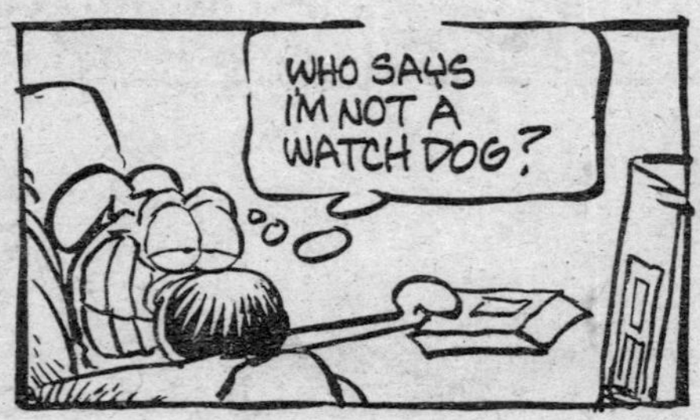
WHO SAYS I'M NOT A WATCH DOG?

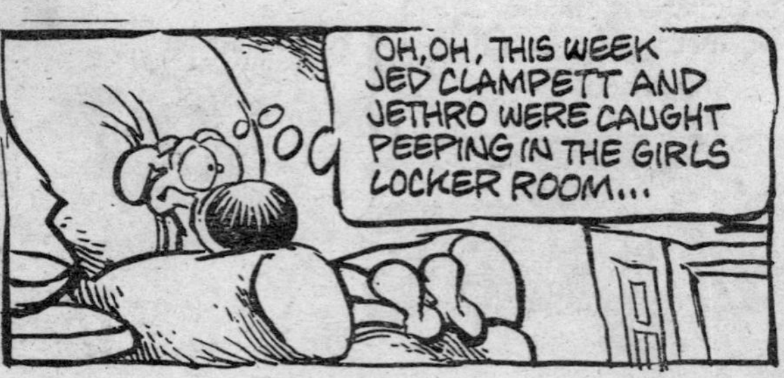
OH, OH, THIS WEEK JED CLAMPETT AND JETHRO WERE CAUGHT PEEPING IN THE GIRLS LOCKER ROOM...

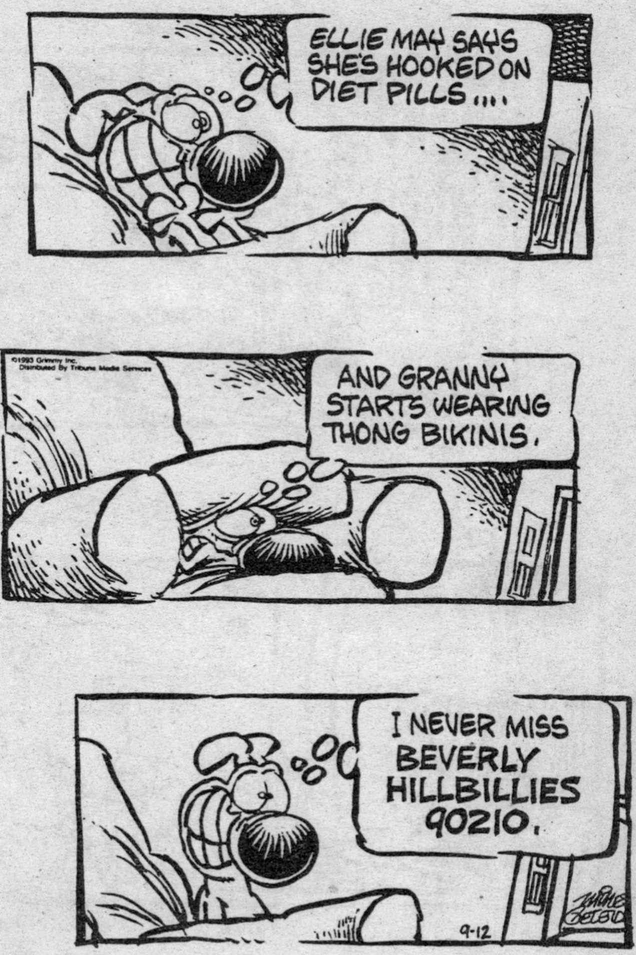
ELLIE MAY SAYS SHE'S HOOKED ON DIET PILLS....
©1993 Grimmy Inc. Distributed By Tribune Media Services
AND GRANNY STARTS WEARING THONG BIKINIS.
I NEVER MISS BEVERLY HILLBILLIES 90210.
9-12

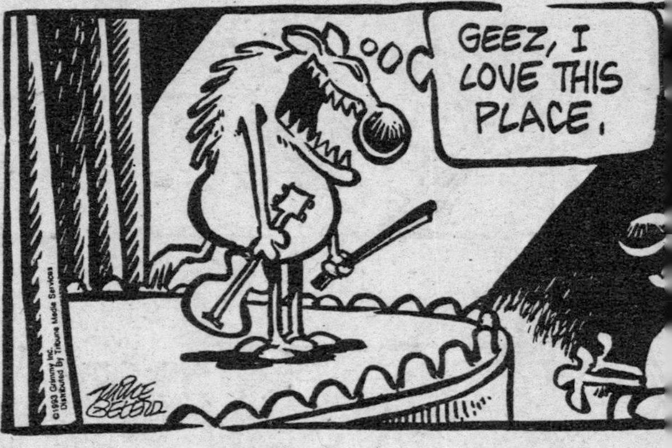
GEEZ, I LOVE THIS PLACE.
©1993 Grimmy Inc. Distributed By Tribune Media Services

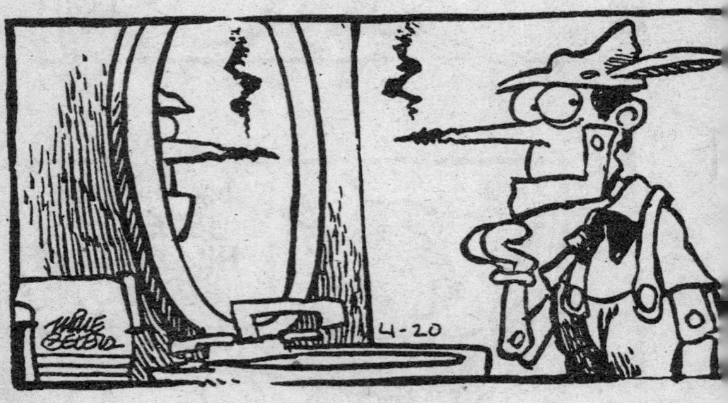
4-20

HYENA COMEDY CLUBS

PINOCCHIO HAD TO EITHER GIVE UP SMOKING OR STOP LYING ABOUT IT.

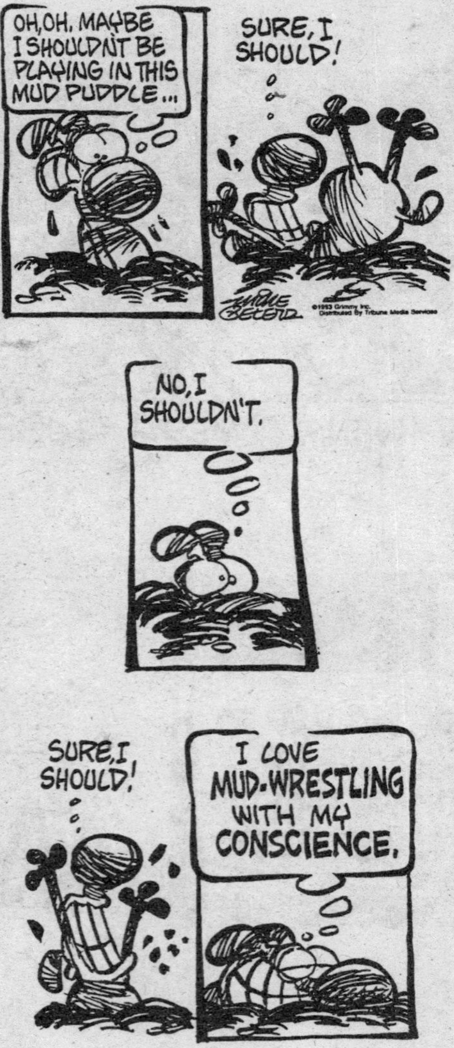
OH,OH. MAYBE I SHOULDN'T BE PLAYING IN THIS MUD PUDDLE...
SURE, I SHOULD!
©1993 Grimmy Inc. Distributed By Tribune Media Services
NO, I SHOULDN'T.
SURE, I SHOULD!
I LOVE MUD-WRESTLING WITH MY CONSCIENCE.

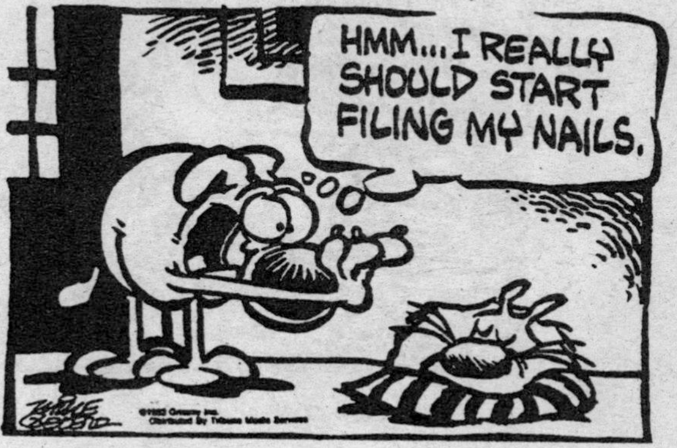
HMM... I REALLY SHOULD START FILING MY NAILS.

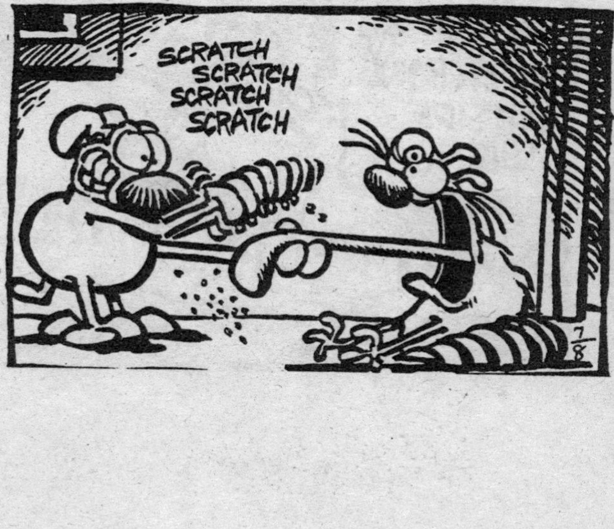
SCRATCH
SCRATCH
SCRATCH
SCRATCH
7/8

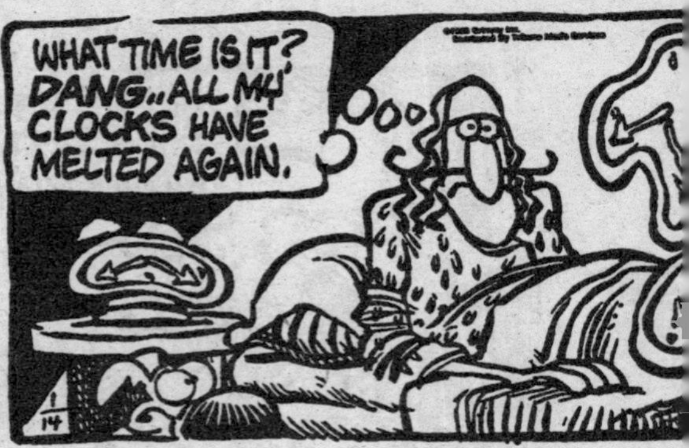
WHAT TIME IS IT? DANG.. ALL MY CLOCKS HAVE MELTED AGAIN.
1/14

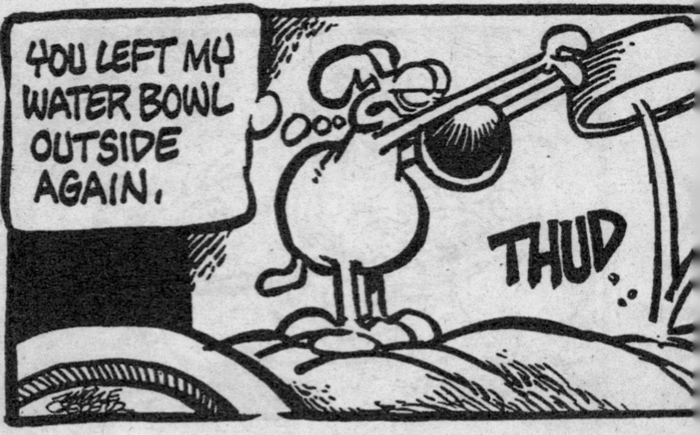
YOU LEFT MY WATER BOWL OUTSIDE AGAIN.
THUD

MORNING AT SALVADOR DALI'S

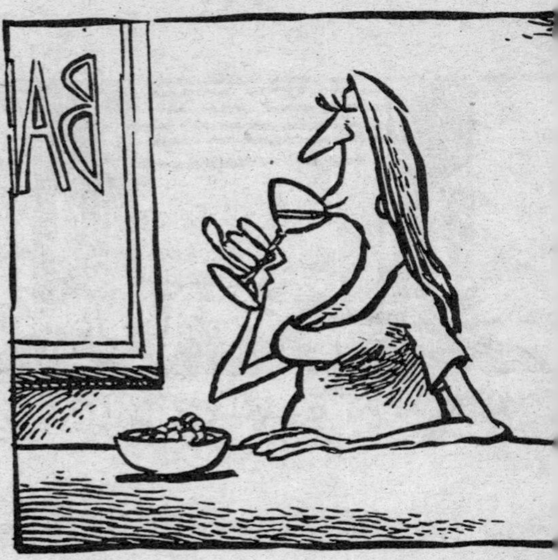

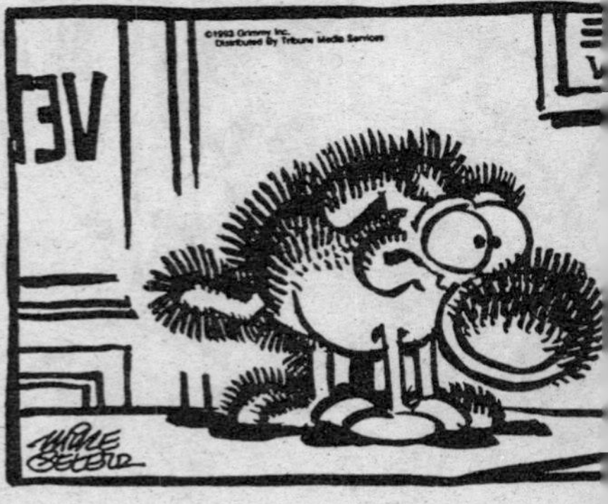
Distributed By Tribune Media Services

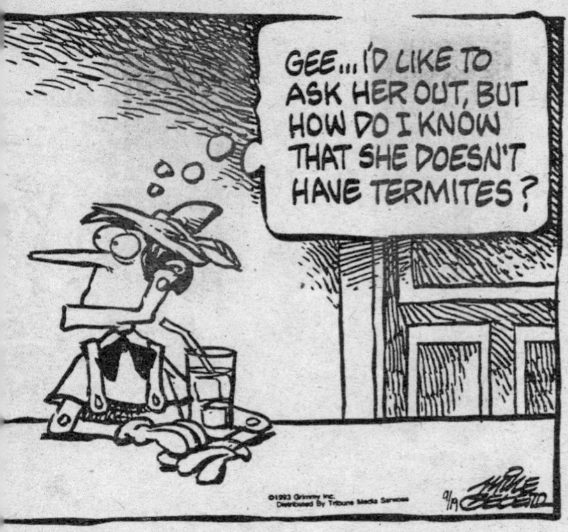
GEE... I'D LIKE TO ASK HER OUT, BUT HOW DO I KNOW THAT SHE DOESN'T HAVE TERMITES?
©1993 Grimmy Inc. Distributed By Tribune Media Services

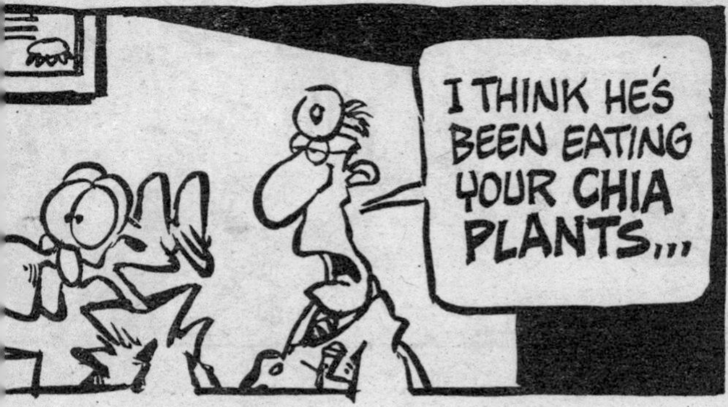
I THINK HE'S BEEN EATING YOUR CHIA PLANTS...

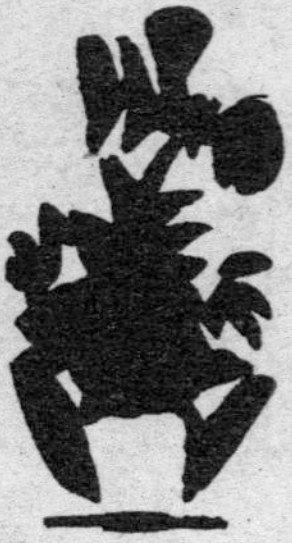

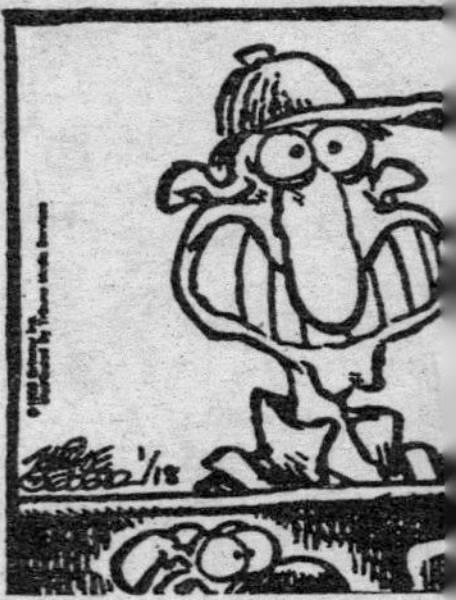

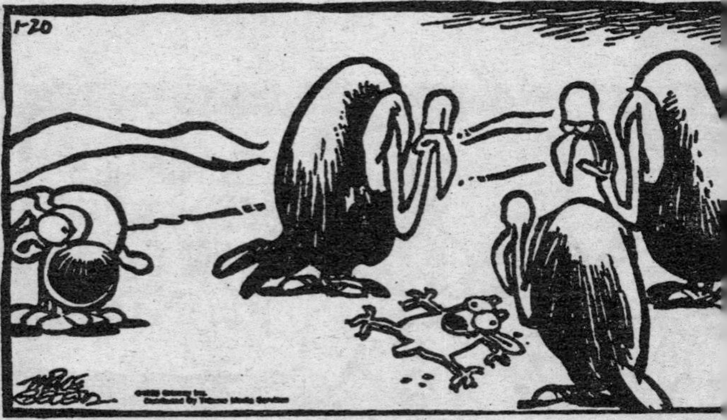

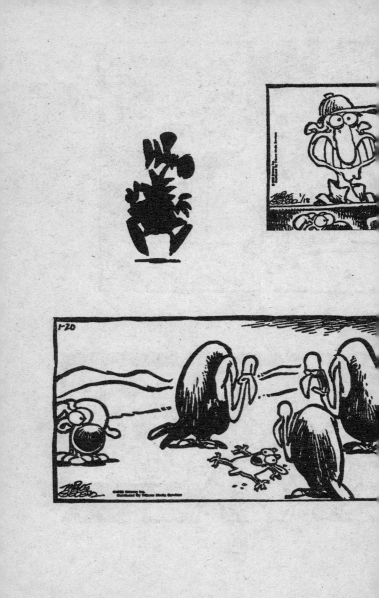

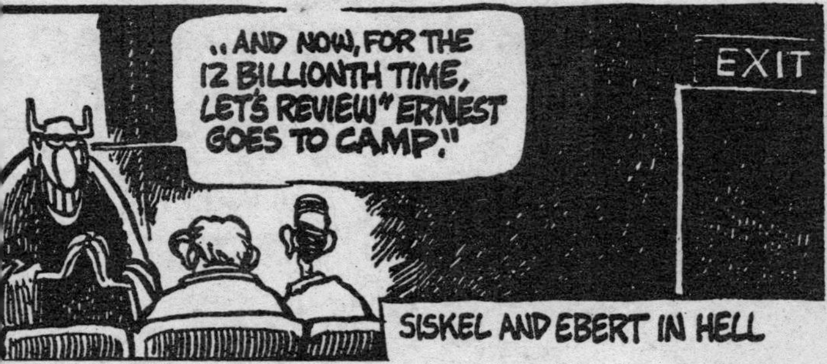
..AND NOW, FOR THE 12 BILLIONTH TIME, LET'S REVIEW "ERNEST GOES TO CAMP."
EXIT

SISKEL AND EBERT IN HELL

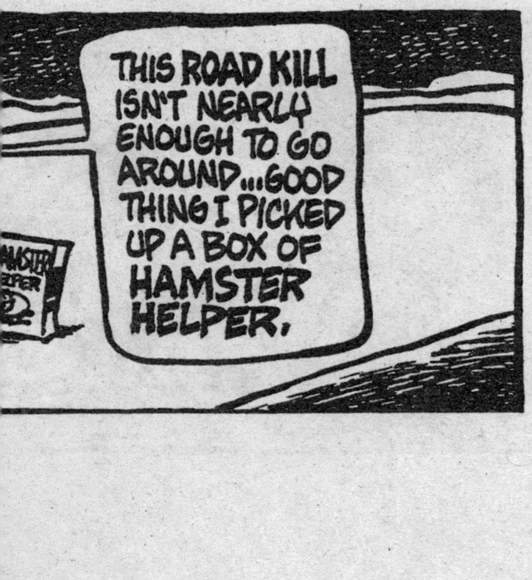
THIS ROAD KILL ISN'T NEARLY ENOUGH TO GO AROUND...GOOD THING I PICKED UP A BOX OF HAMSTER HELPER.

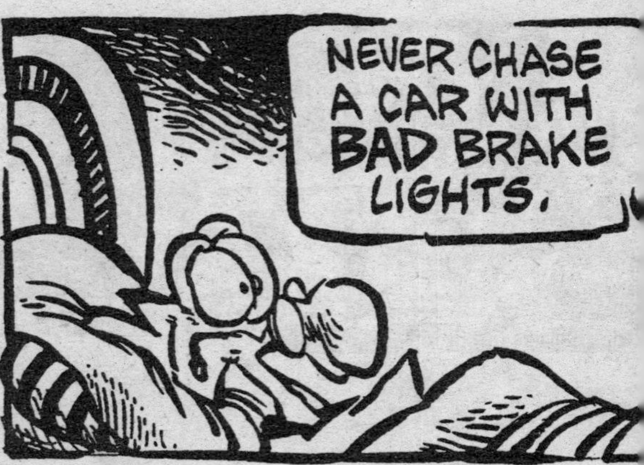
NEVER CHASE A CAR WITH BAD BRAKE LIGHTS.

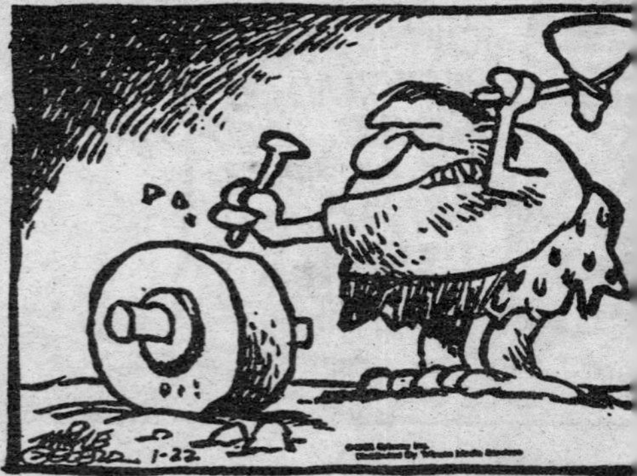
1-22

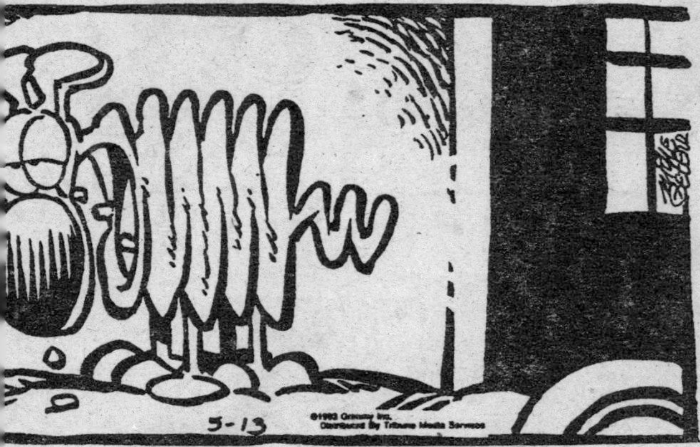
5-13
Distributed By Tribune Media Services

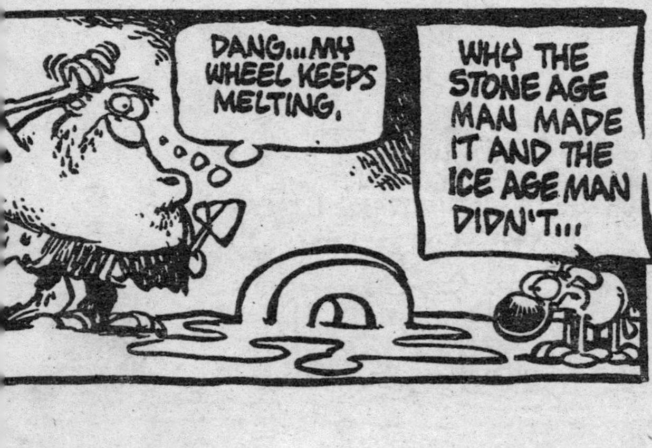
DANG...MY WHEEL KEEPS MELTING.
WHY THE STONE AGE MAN MADE IT AND THE ICE AGE MAN DIDN'T...

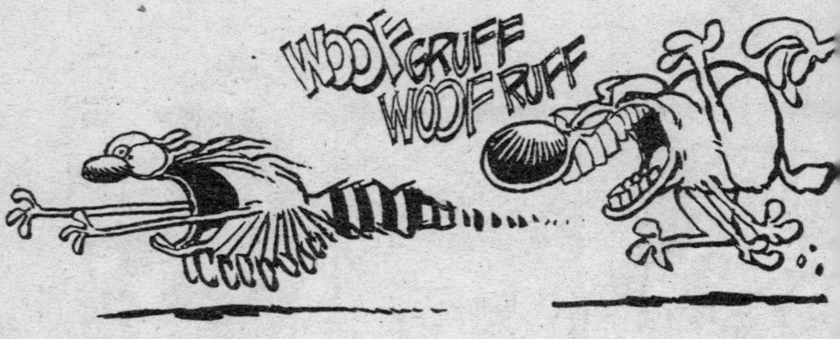
WOOF GRUFF
WOOF RUFF

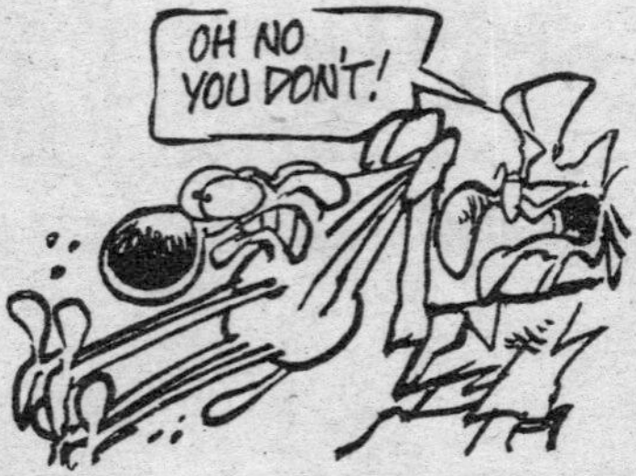
OH NO YOU DON'T!

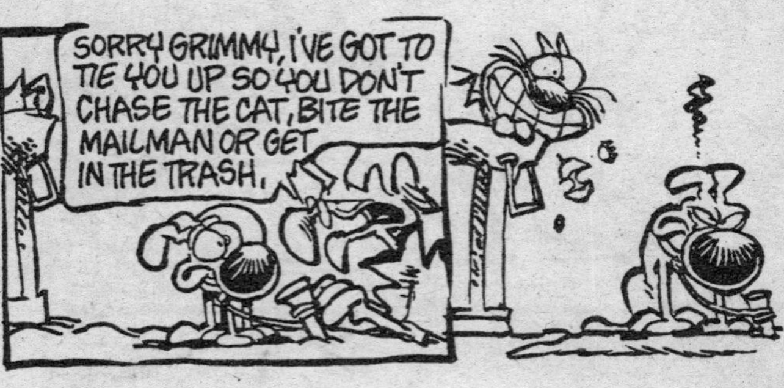
SORRY GRIMMY, I'VE GOT TO TIE YOU UP SO YOU DON'T CHASE THE CAT, BITE THE MAILMAN OR GET IN THE TRASH.

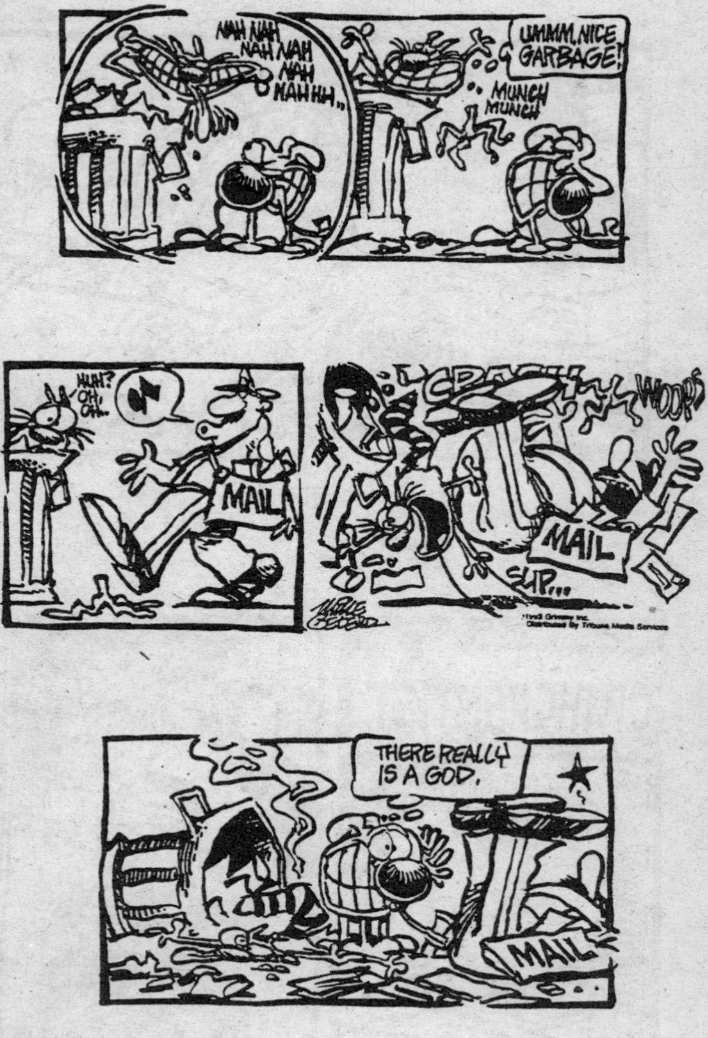
NAH NAH NAH NAH NAH NAHHH..
UMMM, NICE GARBAGE!
MUNCH MUNCH
HUH? OH, OH..
CRASH
WOOPS
MAIL
MAIL
SLIP...
Grimmy Inc.
Distributed By Tribune Media Services
THERE REALLY IS A GOD.
MAIL

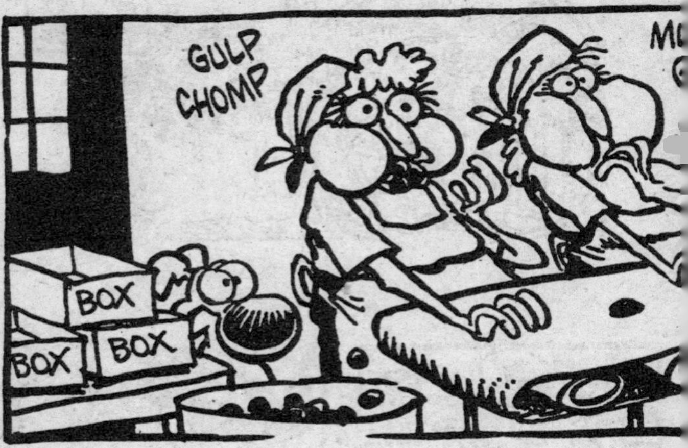
GULP
CHOMP
BOX
BOX
BOX

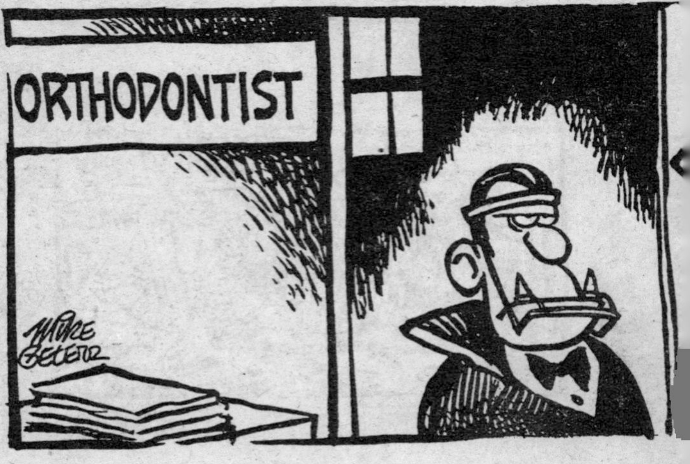
ORTHODONTIST
MIKE PETERS

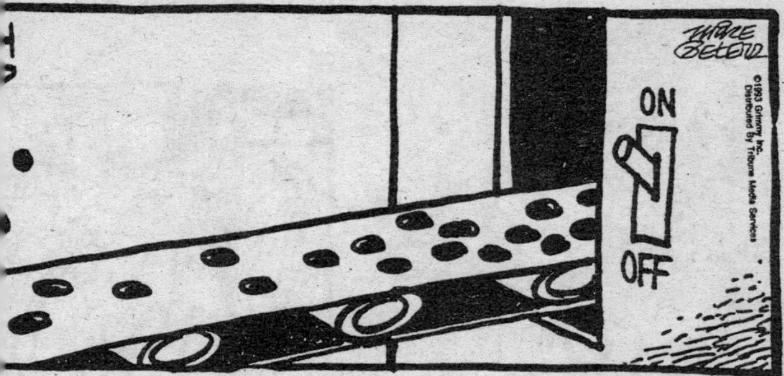
ON
OFF
©1993 Grimmy, Inc.
Distributed By Tribune Media Services

LUCY AND ETHYL BEGIN THEIR FIRST AND LAST DAY AT THE LAXATIVE FACTORY

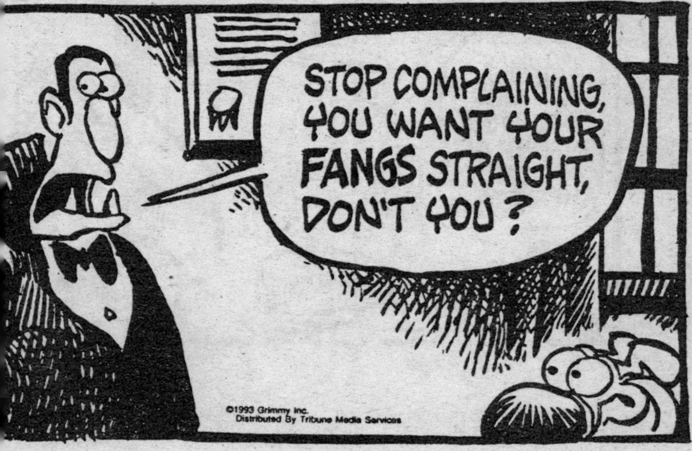
STOP COMPLAINING, YOU WANT YOUR FANGS STRAIGHT, DON'T YOU?
©1993 Grimmy Inc.
Distributed By Tribune Media Services

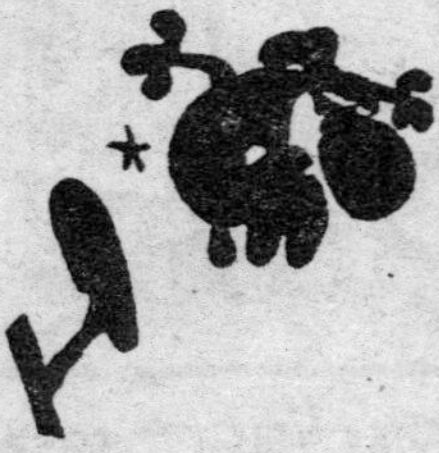

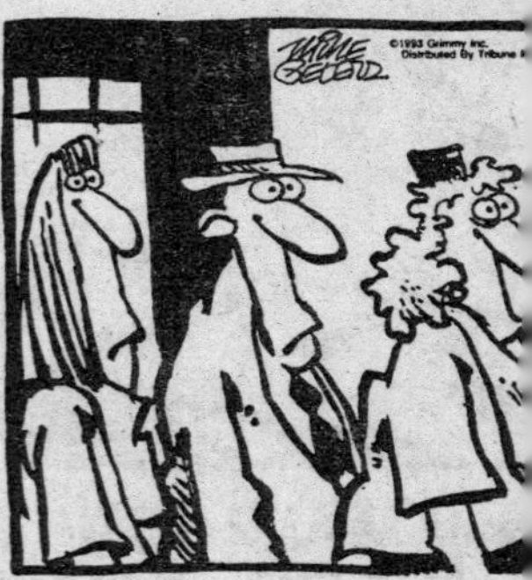
©1993 Grimmy Inc.
Distributed By Tribune

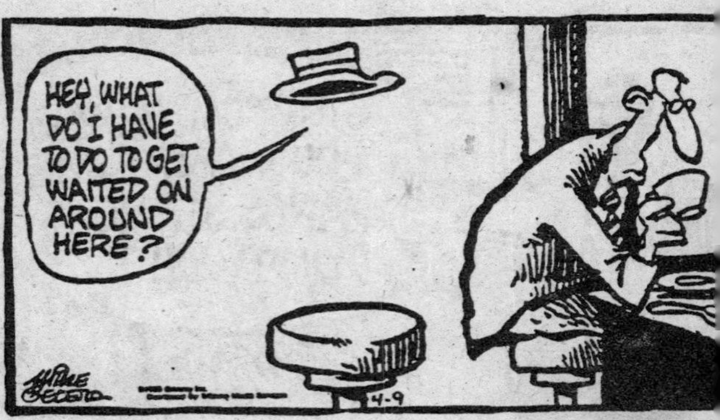
HEY, WHAT DO I HAVE TO DO TO GET WAITED ON AROUND HERE?
4-9

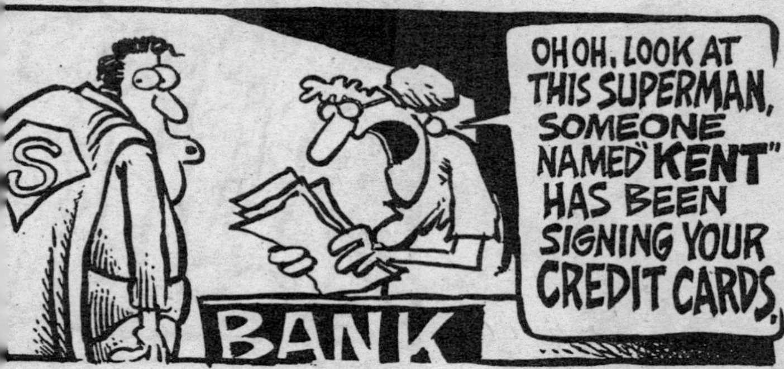
OH OH, LOOK AT THIS SUPERMAN, SOMEONE NAMED "KENT" HAS BEEN SIGNING YOUR CREDIT CARDS.
BANK

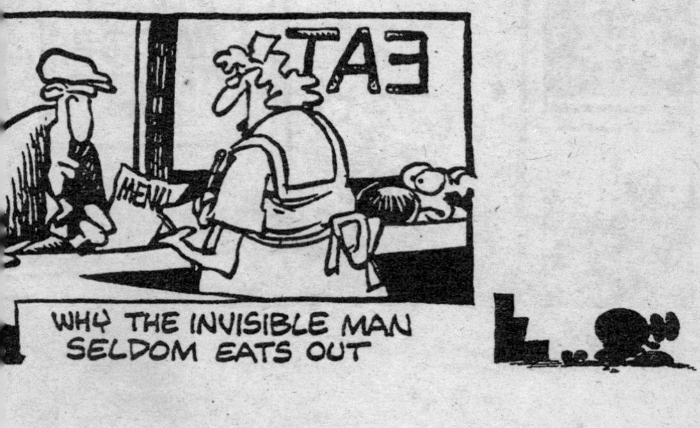
EAT
MENU
WHY THE INVISIBLE MAN SELDOM EATS OUT

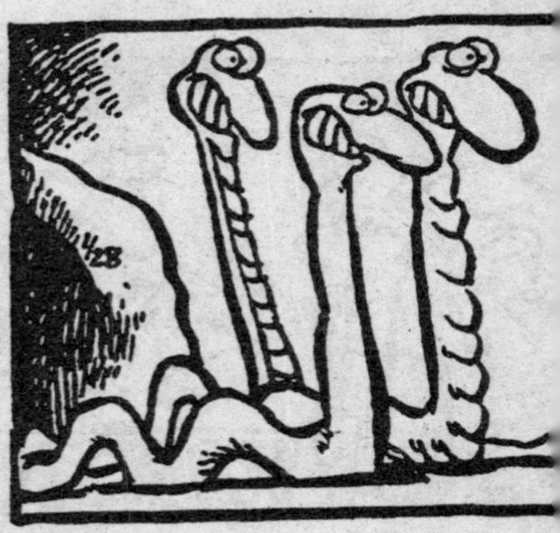

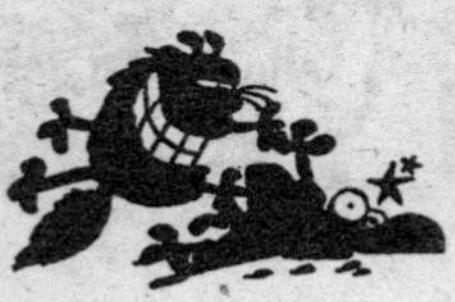

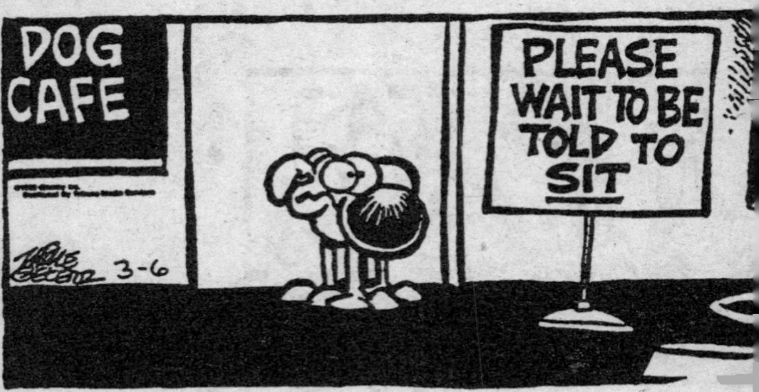
DOG
CAFE
3-6
PLEASE
WAIT TO BE
TOLD TO
SIT

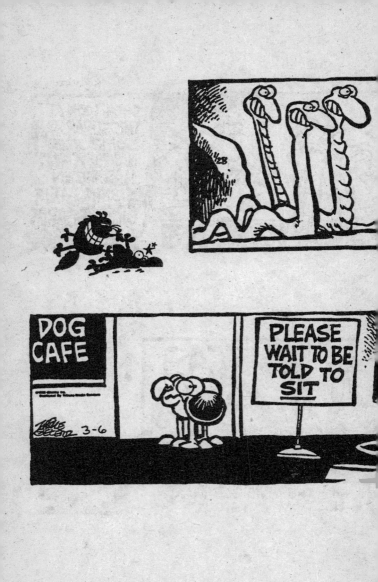

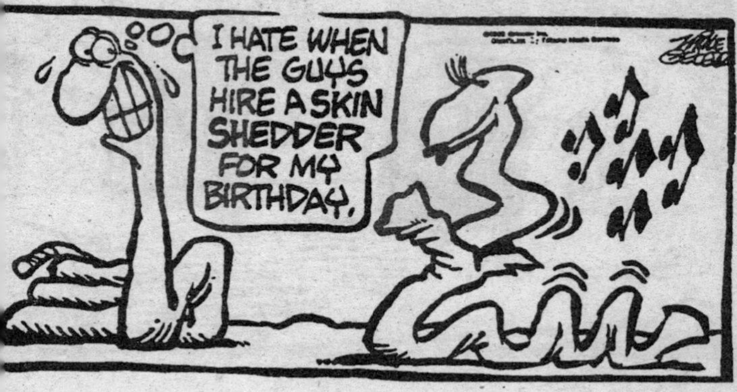
I HATE WHEN THE GUYS HIRE A SKIN SHEDDER FOR MY BIRTHDAY.

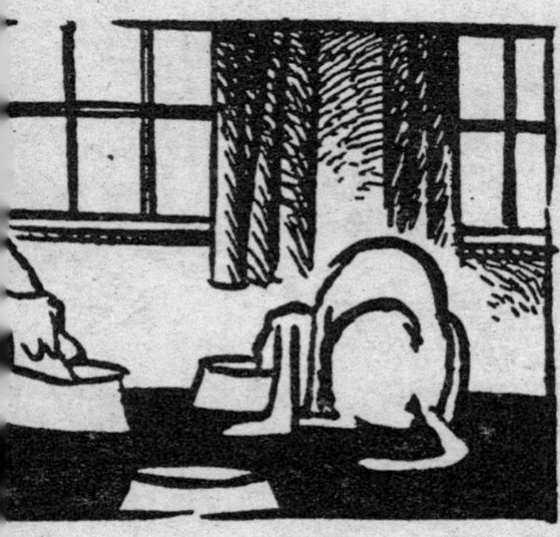

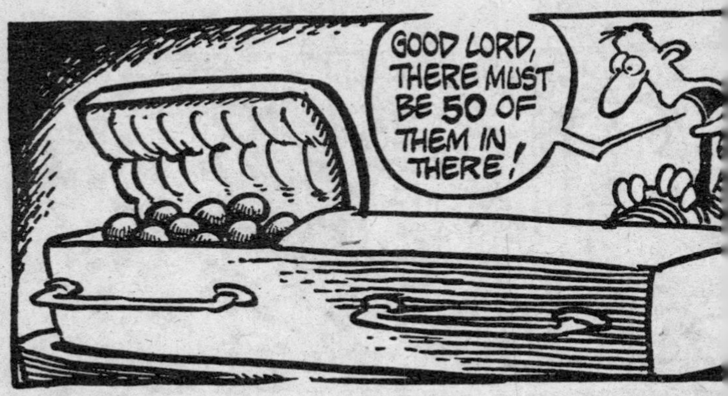
GOOD LORD, THERE MUST BE 50 OF THEM IN THERE!

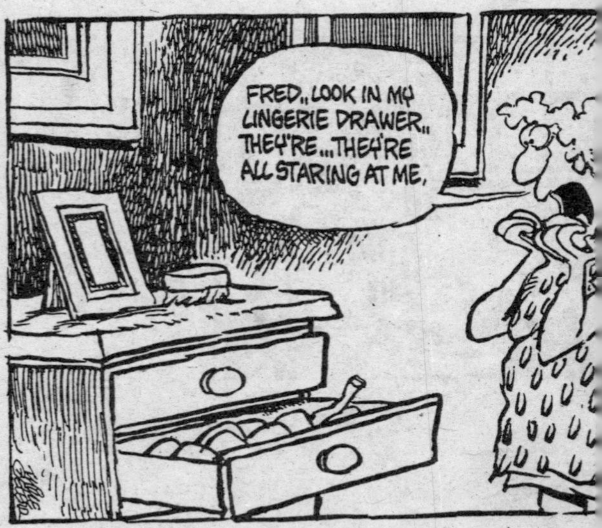
FRED.. LOOK IN MY LINGERIE DRAWER.. THEY'RE...THEY'RE ALL STARING AT ME.

CLOWN FUNERALS

NIGHT OF THE LIVING BRAS

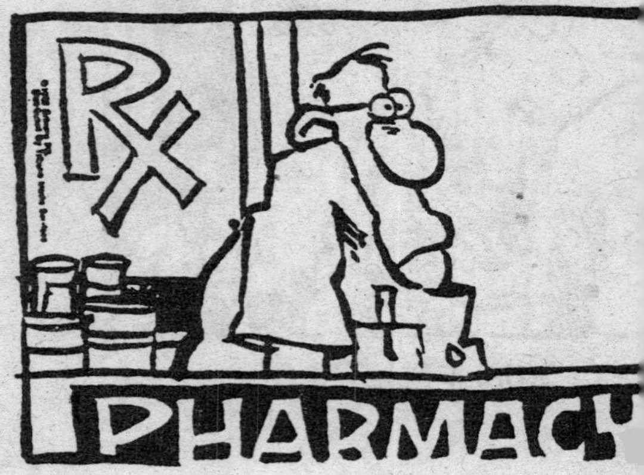

Rx
PHARMAC

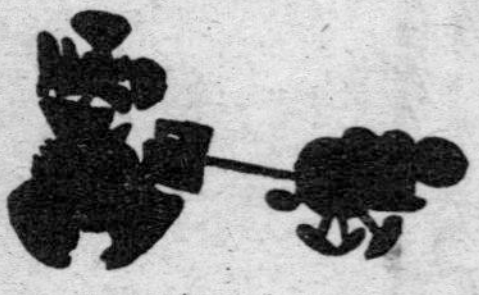

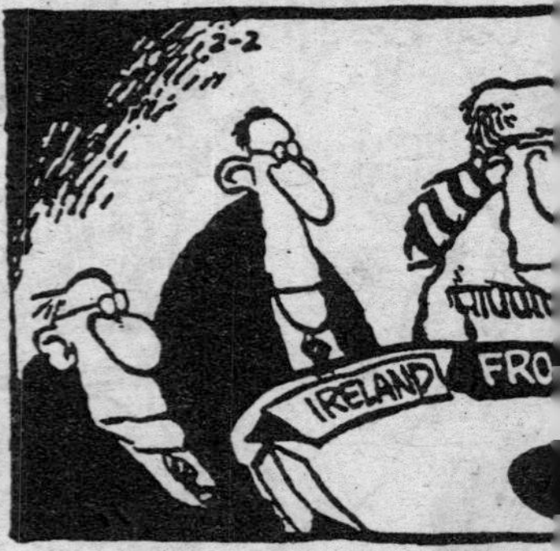

IRELAND
FRO

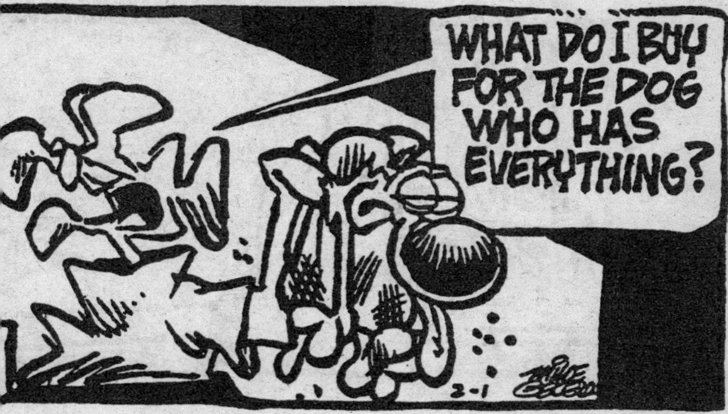
WHAT DO I BUY FOR THE DOG WHO HAS EVERYTHING?

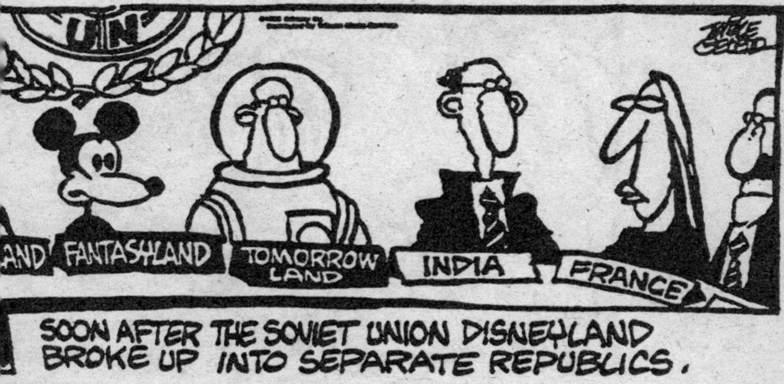
UN
AND
FANTASYLAND
TOMORROW LAND
INDIA
FRANCE

SOON AFTER THE SOVIET UNION DISNEYLAND BROKE UP INTO SEPARATE REPUBLICS.

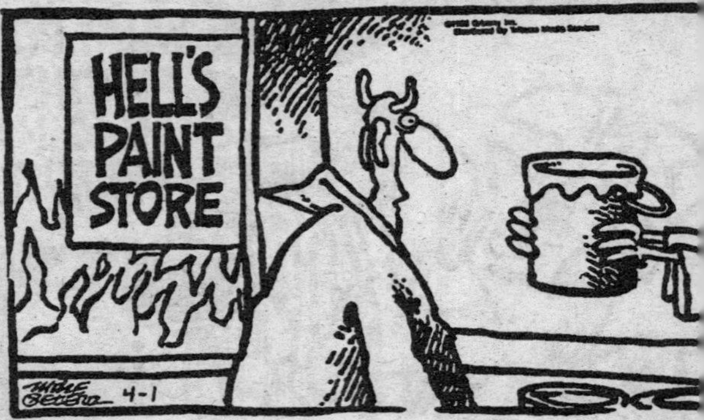
HELL'S
PAINT
STORE
4-1

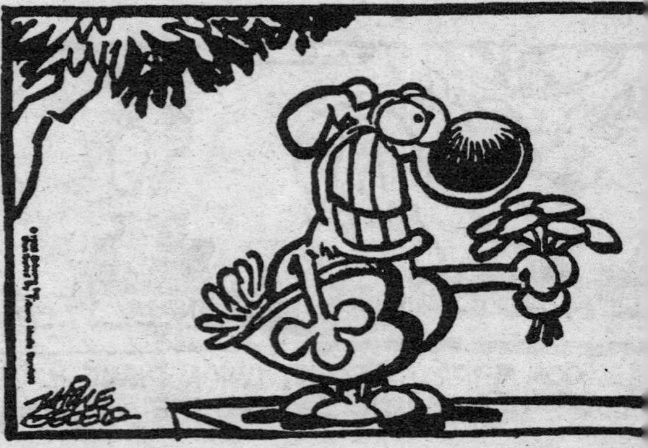

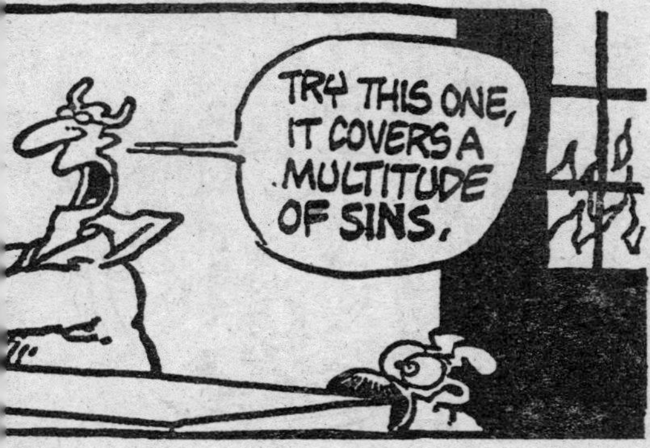
TRY THIS ONE, IT COVERS A MULTITUDE OF SINS.

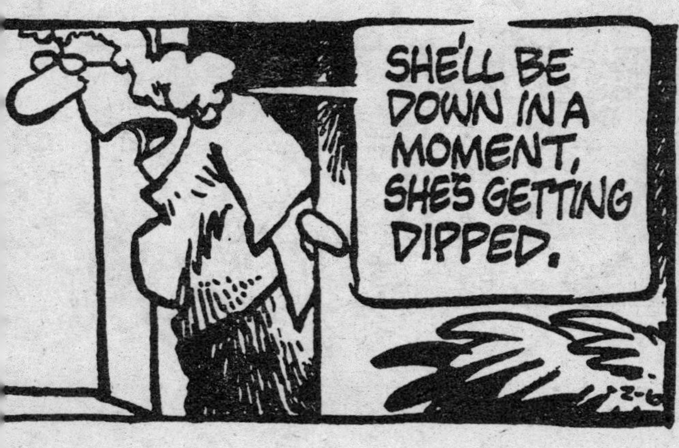
SHE'LL BE DOWN IN A MOMENT, SHE'S GETTING DIPPED.

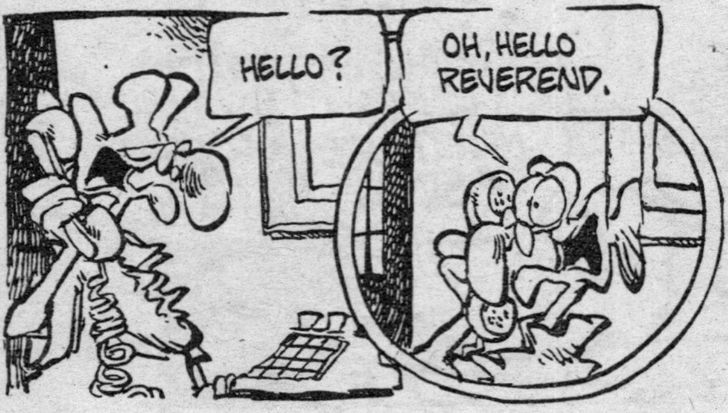
HELLO?
OH, HELLO REVEREND.

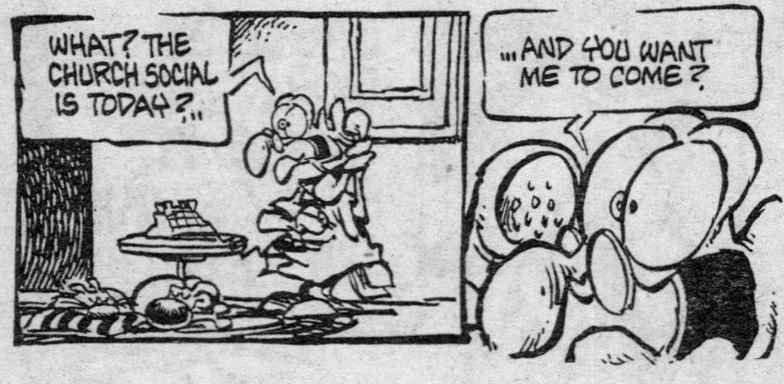
WHAT? THE CHURCH SOCIAL IS TODAY?...
...AND YOU WANT ME TO COME?

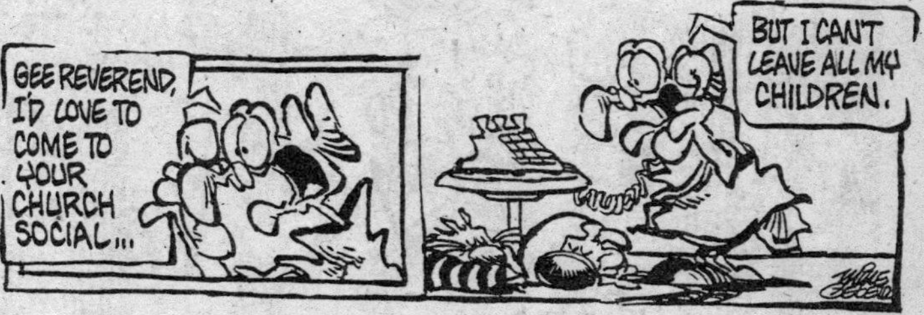
GEE REVEREND, I'D LOVE TO COME TO YOUR CHURCH SOCIAL...
BUT I CAN'T LEAVE ALL MY CHILDREN.

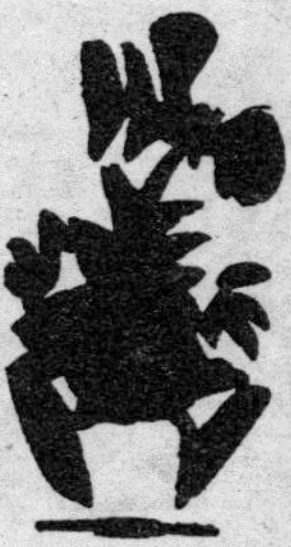

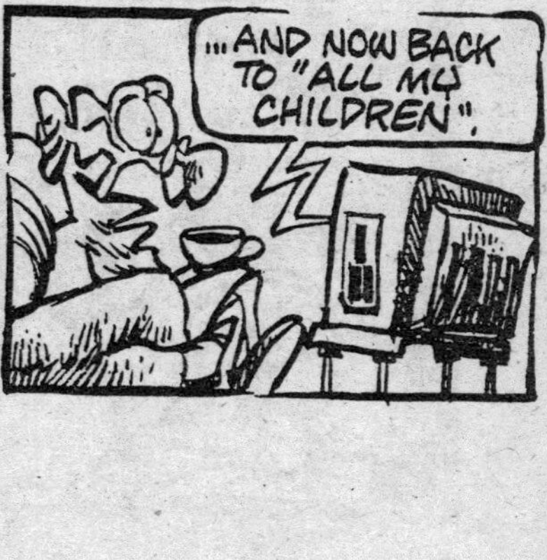
...AND NOW BACK TO "ALL MY CHILDREN".

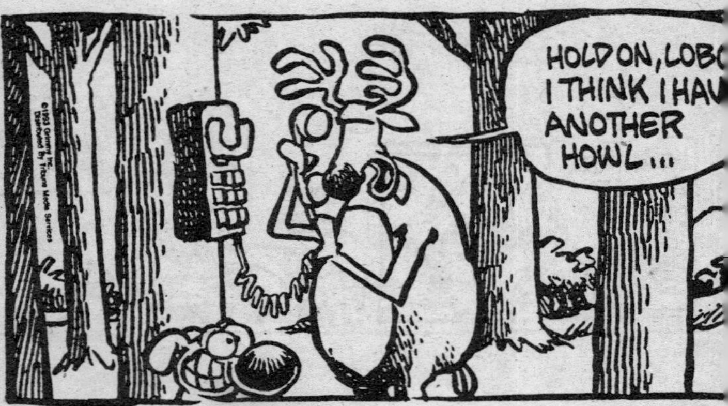
HOLD ON, LOB
I THINK I HAV
ANOTHER
HOWL...
©1993 Grimmy Inc.
Distributed by Tribune Media Services

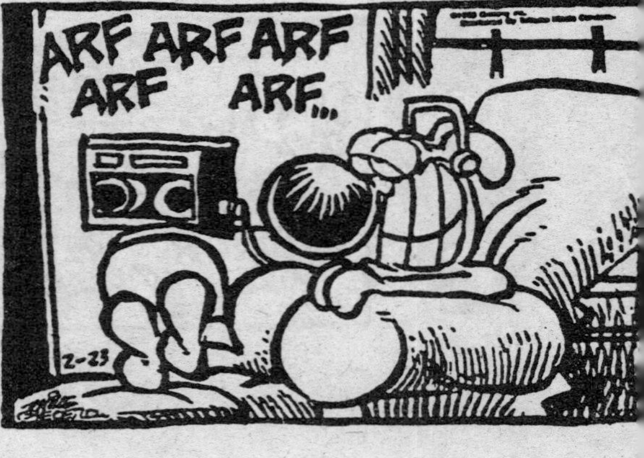
ARF ARF ARF
ARF ARF...
2-23

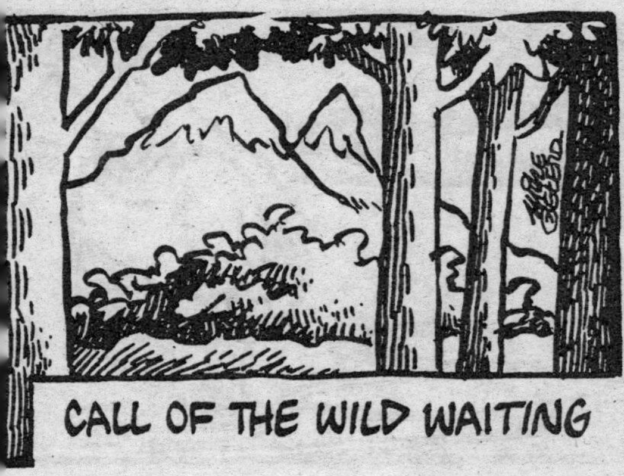
CALL OF THE WILD WAITING

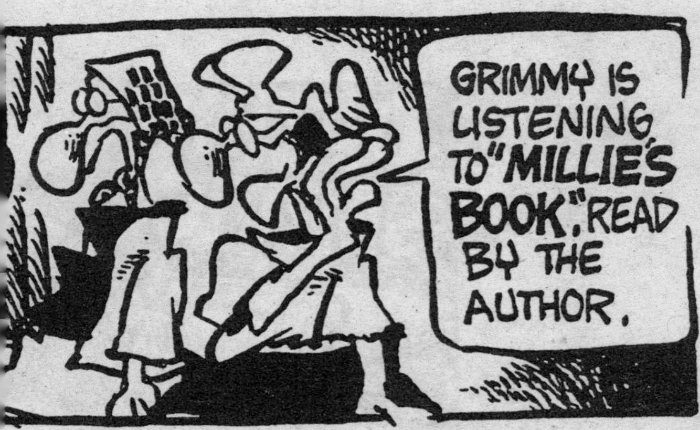
GRIMMY IS LISTENING TO "MILLIE'S BOOK," READ BY THE AUTHOR.

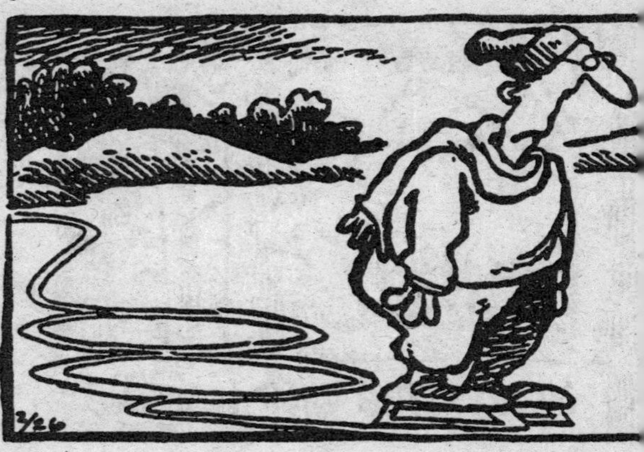
3/26

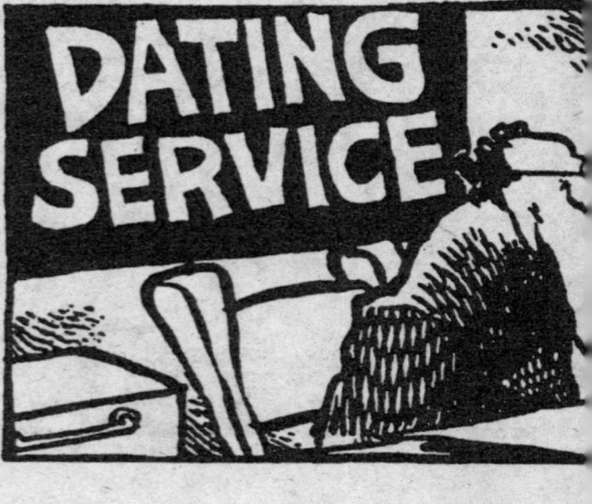
DATING SERVICE

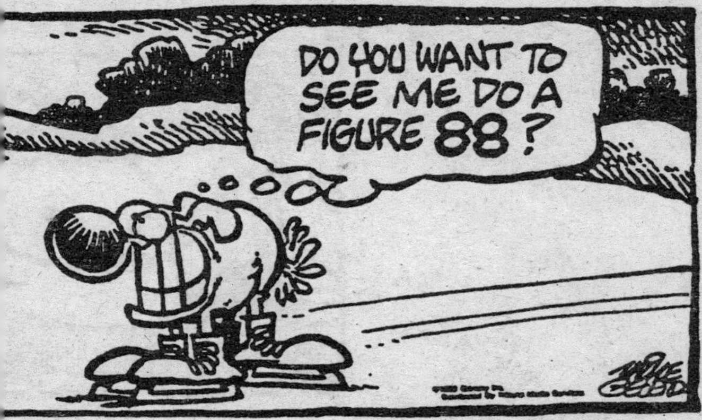
DO YOU WANT TO SEE ME DO A FIGURE 88?

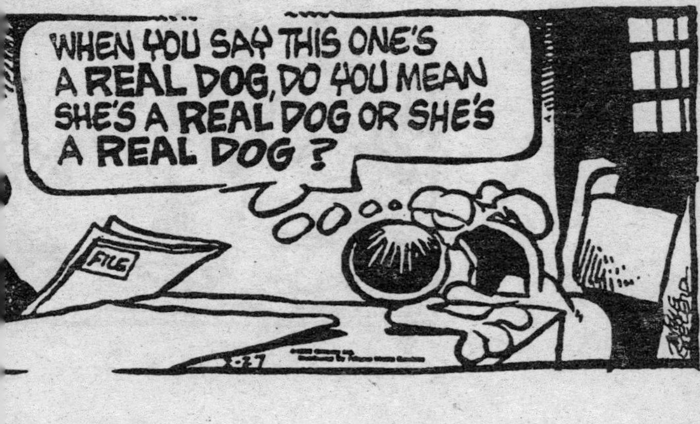
WHEN YOU SAY THIS ONE'S A REAL DOG, DO YOU MEAN SHE'S A REAL DOG OR SHE'S A REAL DOG?
FILE

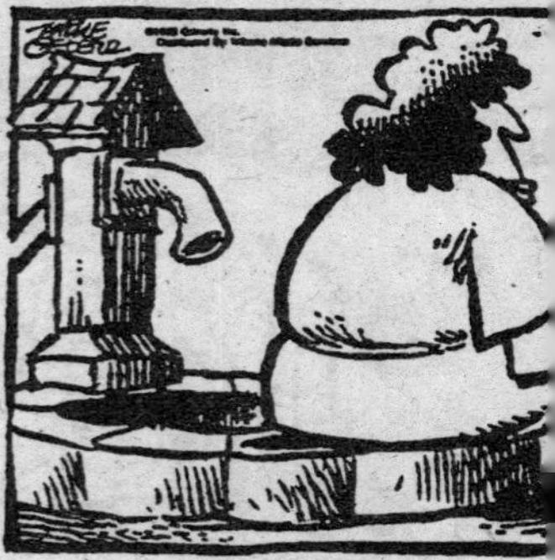

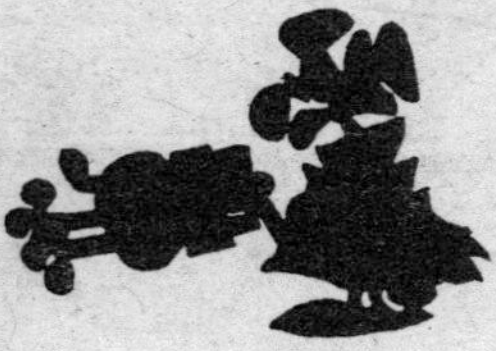

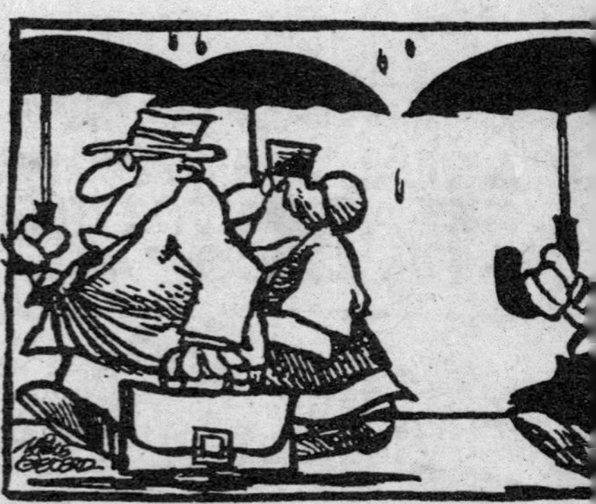

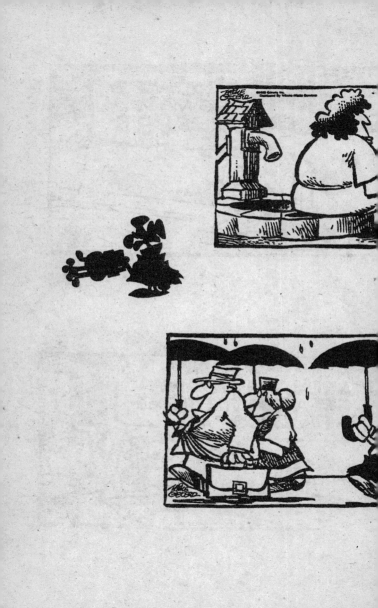

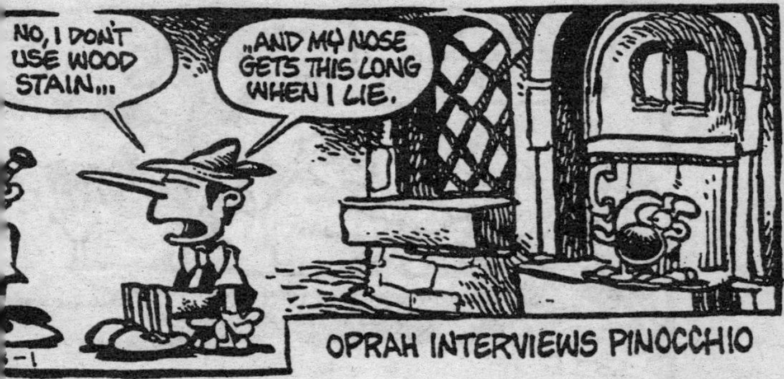
NO, I DON'T USE WOOD STAIN...
..AND MY NOSE GETS THIS LONG WHEN I LIE.
OPRAH INTERVIEWS PINOCCHIO

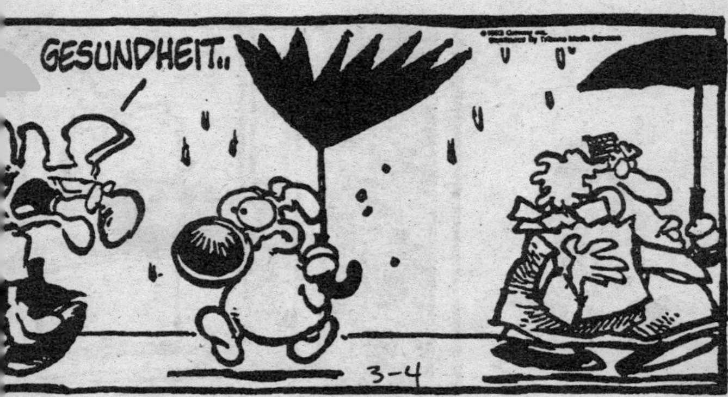
GESUNDHEIT..
3-4

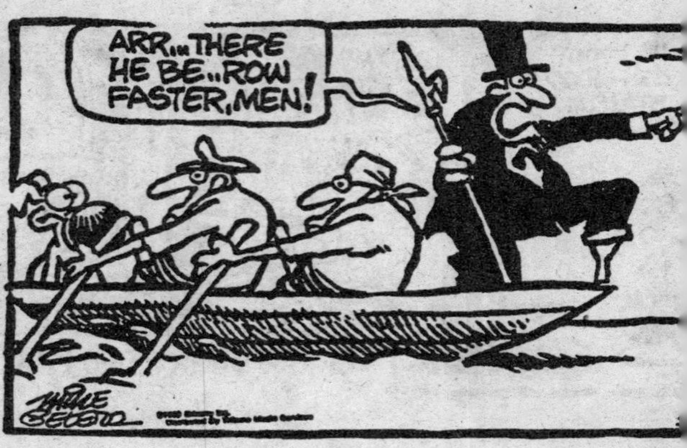
ARR..THERE HE BE..ROW FASTER, MEN!

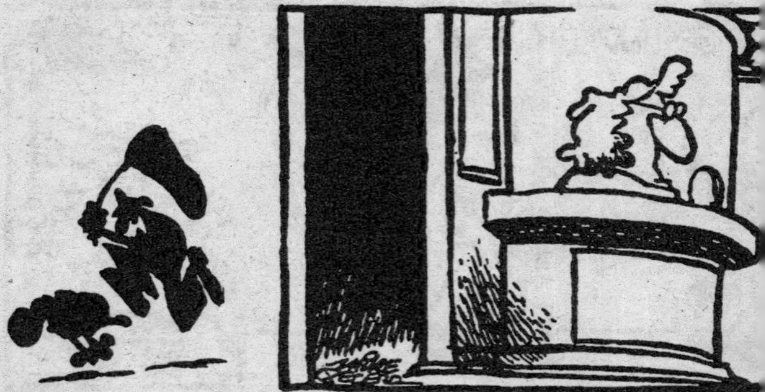

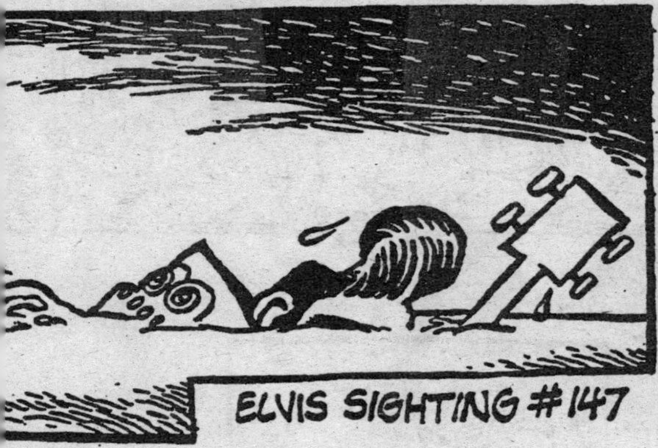
ELVIS SIGHTING #147

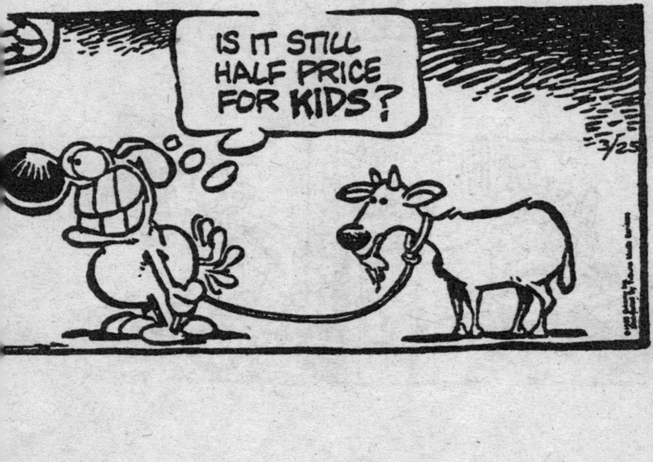
IS IT STILL HALF PRICE FOR KIDS?
3/25

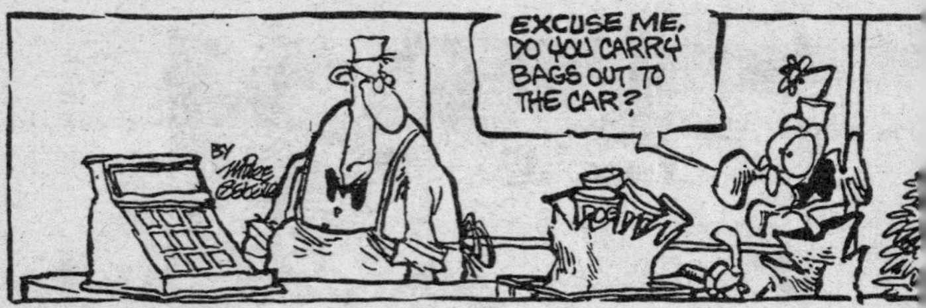
EXCUSE ME, DO YOU CARRY BAGS OUT TO THE CAR?

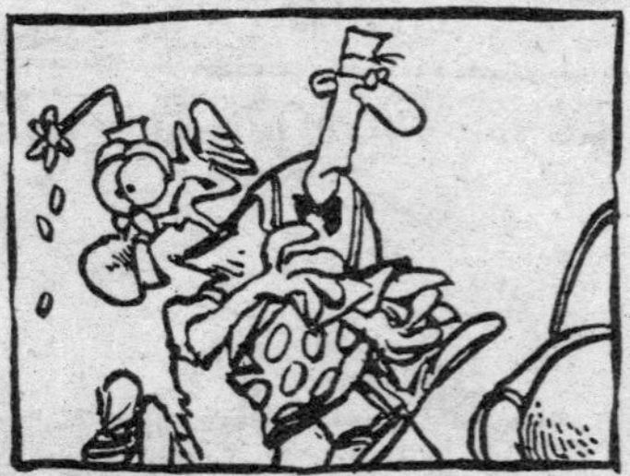

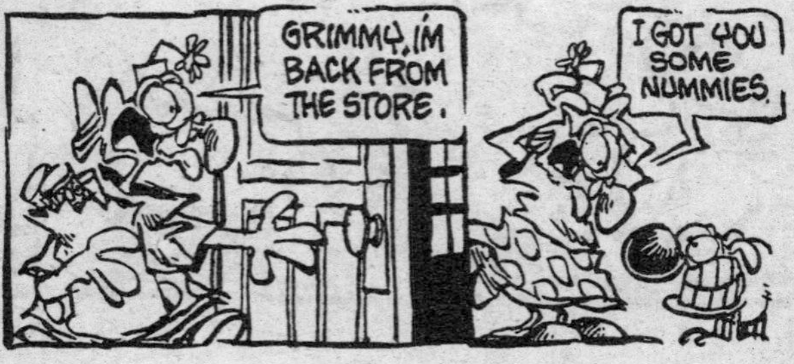
GRIMMY, I'M BACK FROM THE STORE.
I GOT YOU SOME NUMMIES.

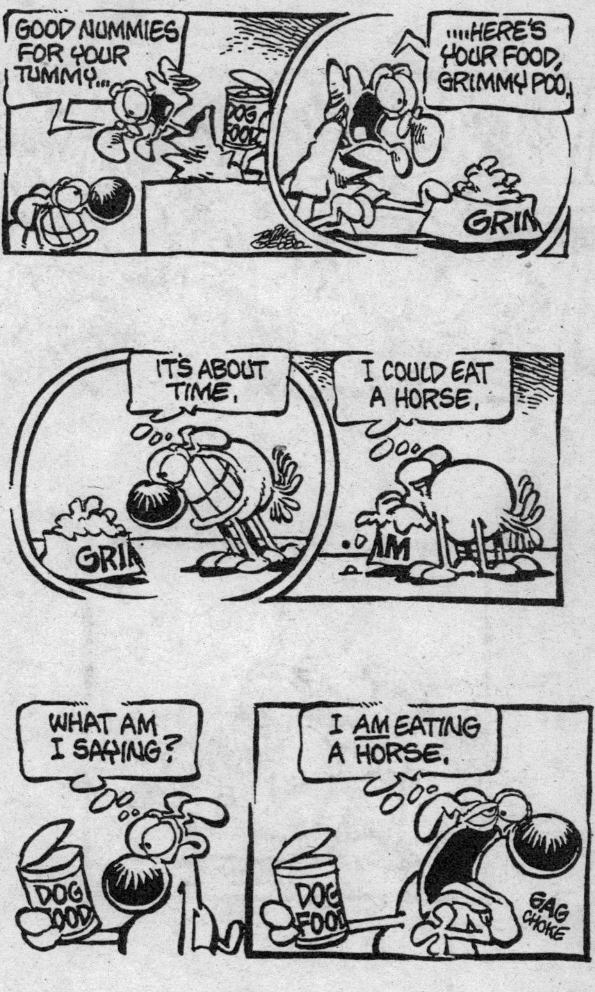
GOOD NUMMIES FOR YOUR TUMMY...
DOG FOOD
....HERE'S YOUR FOOD, GRIMMY POO.
IT'S ABOUT TIME.
I COULD EAT A HORSE.
WHAT AM I SAYING?
DOG FOOD
I AM EATING A HORSE.
DOG FOOD
GAG CHOKE

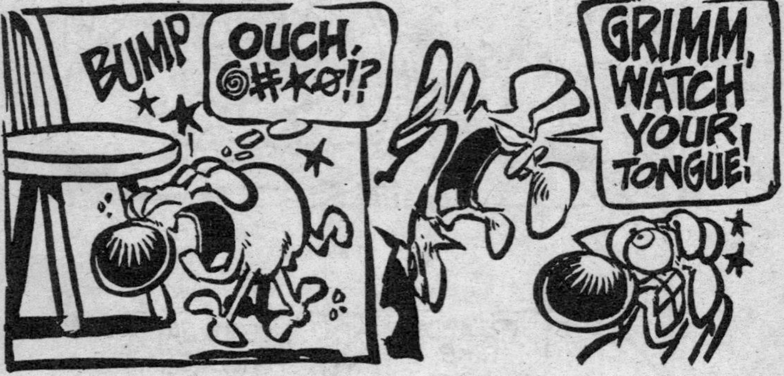
BUMP
OUCH, @#*&!?
GRIMM, WATCH YOUR TONGUE!

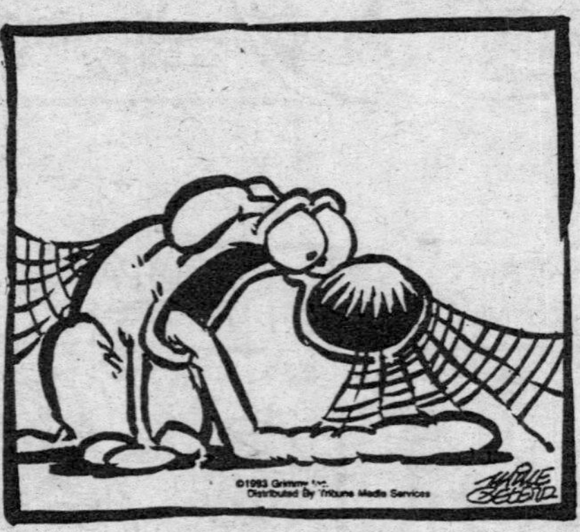
©1993 Grimmy
Distributed By Tribune Media Services

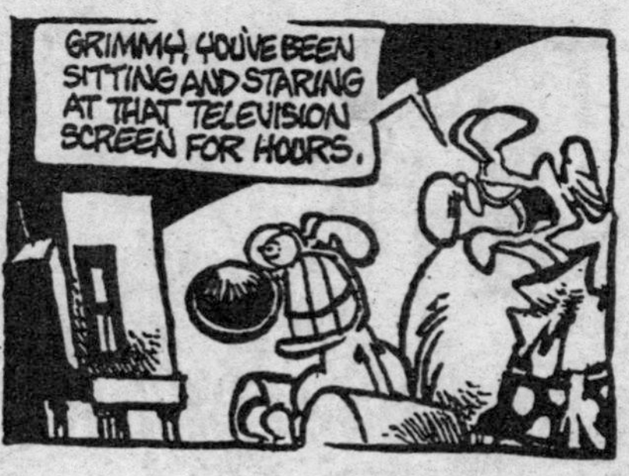
GRIMMY, YOU'VE BEEN SITTING AND STARING AT THAT TELEVISION SCREEN FOR HOURS.

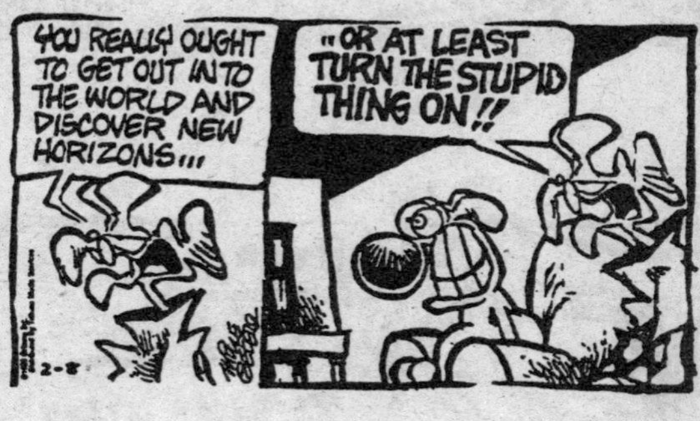
YOU REALLY OUGHT TO GET OUT INTO THE WORLD AND DISCOVER NEW HORIZONS...
...OR AT LEAST TURN THE STUPID THING ON!!
2-8

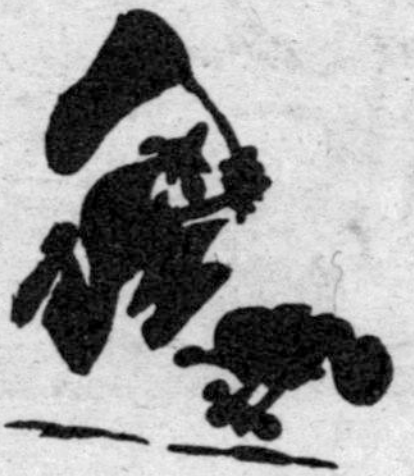

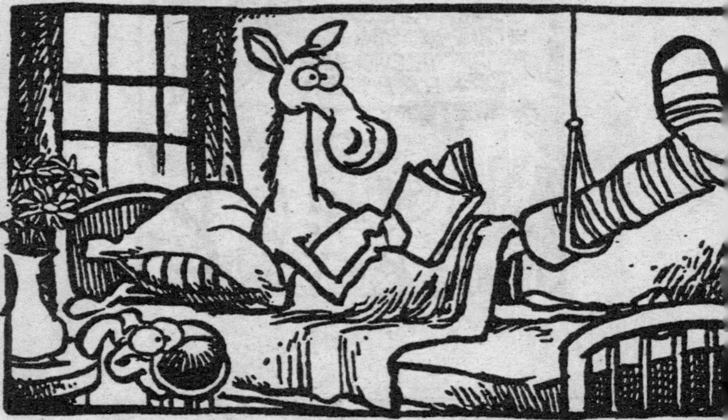

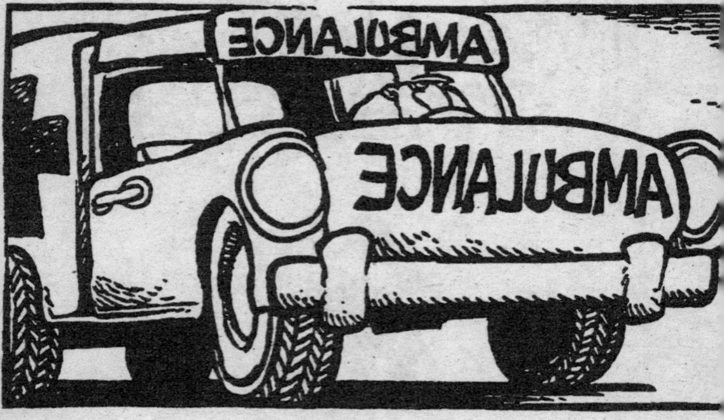
AMBULANCE
AMBULANCE

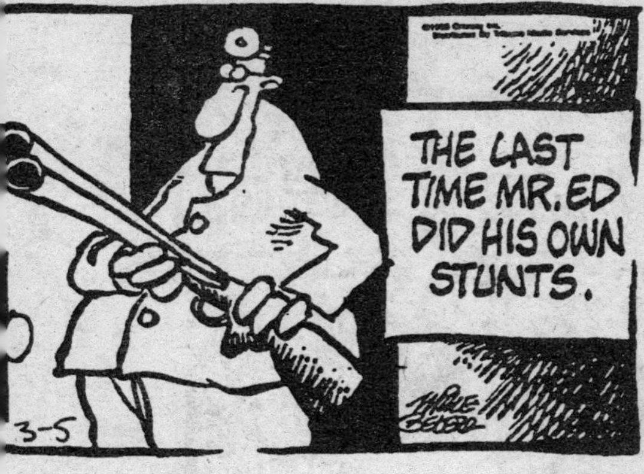
THE LAST TIME MR. ED DID HIS OWN STUNTS.
3-5

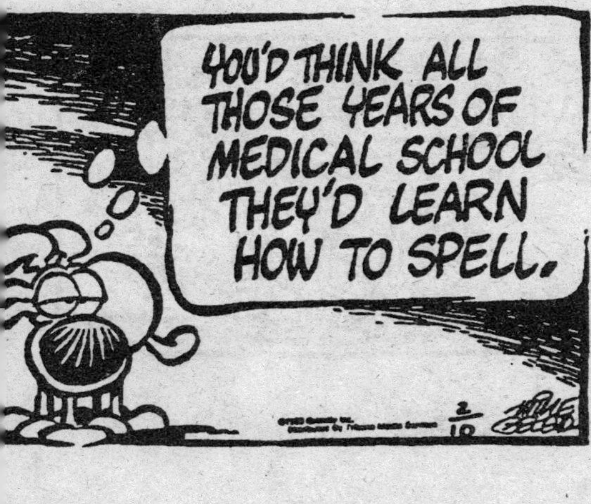
YOU'D THINK ALL THOSE YEARS OF MEDICAL SCHOOL THEY'D LEARN HOW TO SPELL.
2/10

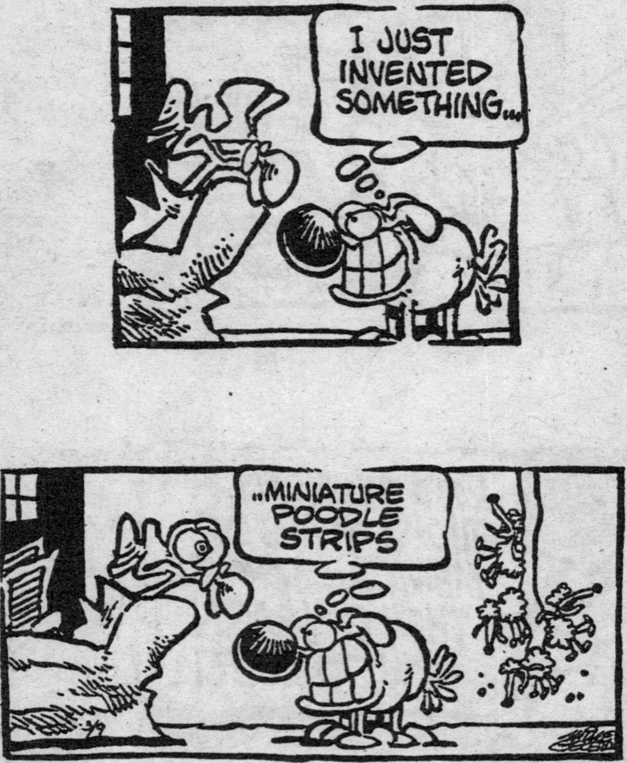
I JUST INVENTED SOMETHING...
..MINIATURE POODLE STRIPS

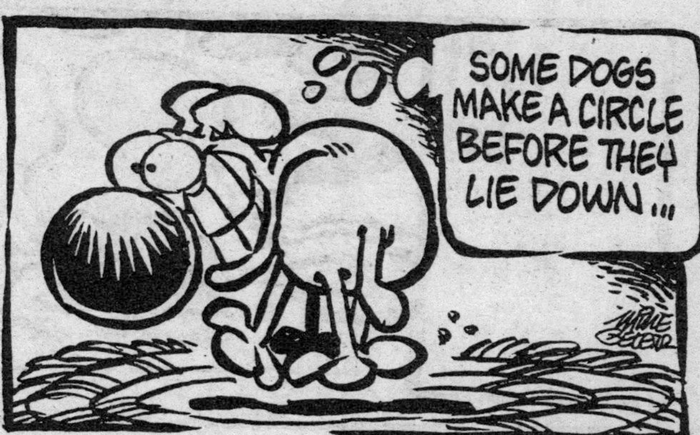
SOME DOGS MAKE A CIRCLE BEFORE THEY LIE DOWN...

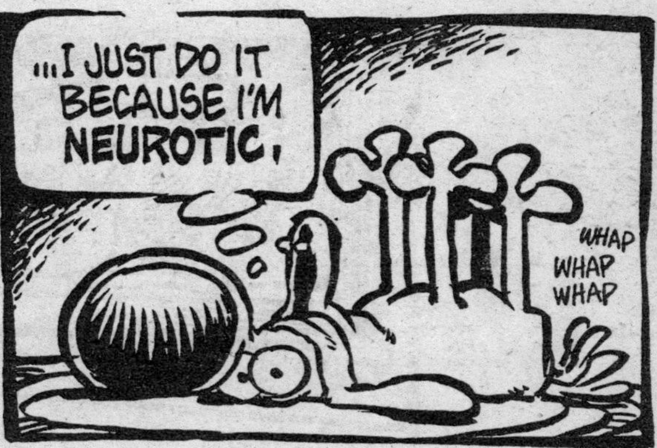
...I JUST DO IT BECAUSE I'M NEUROTIC.
WHAP
WHAP
WHAP

2-13

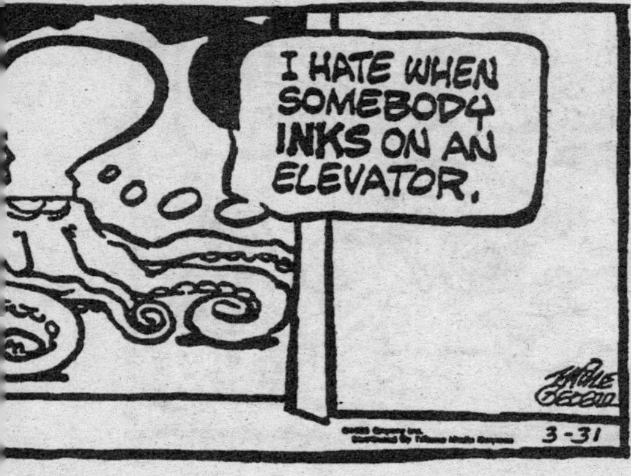
I HATE WHEN SOMEBODY INKS ON AN ELEVATOR.
3-31

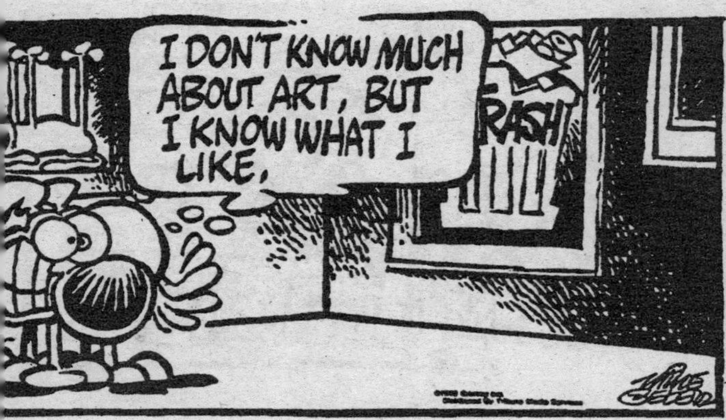
I DON'T KNOW MUCH ABOUT ART, BUT I KNOW WHAT I LIKE.
RASH

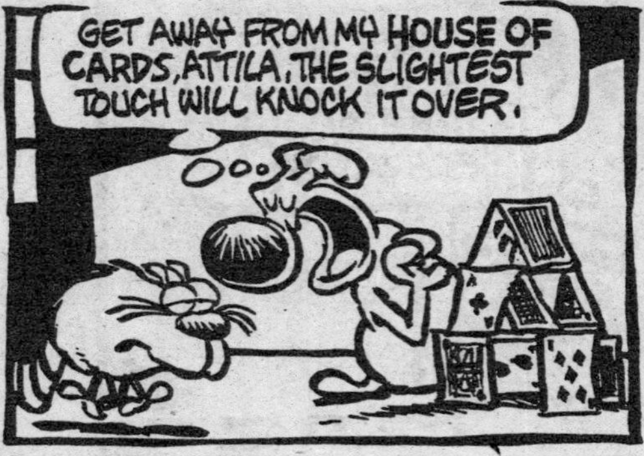
GET AWAY FROM MY HOUSE OF CARDS, ATTILA, THE SLIGHTEST TOUCH WILL KNOCK IT OVER.

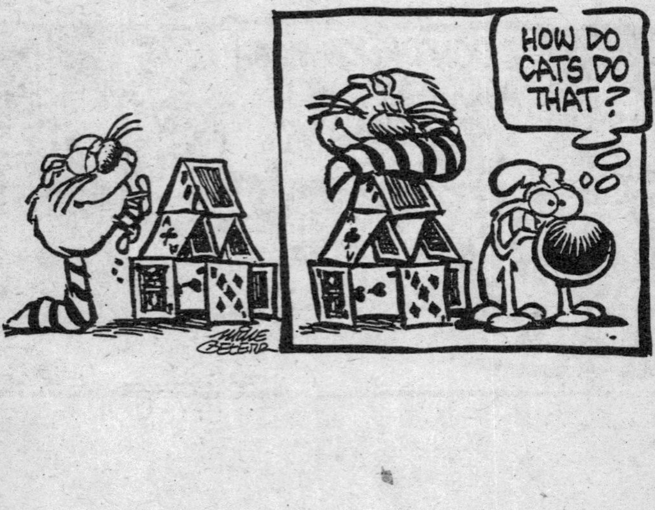
HOW DO CATS DO THAT?

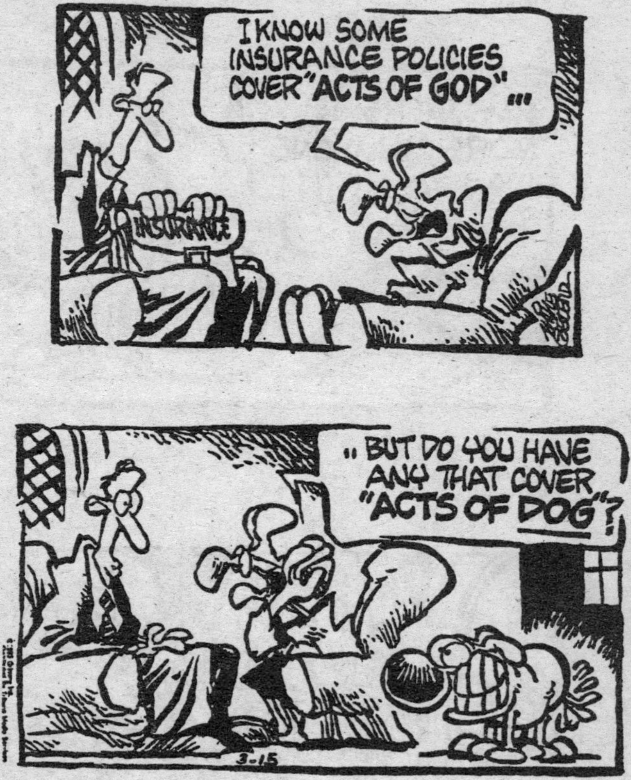
I KNOW SOME INSURANCE POLICIES COVER "ACTS OF GOD"...
INSURANCE
... BUT DO YOU HAVE ANY THAT COVER "ACTS OF DOG"?
3-15

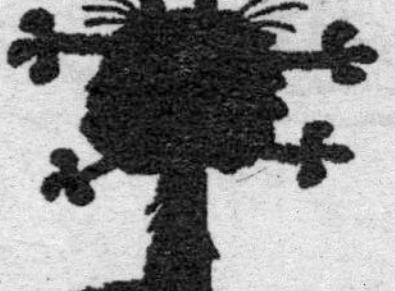

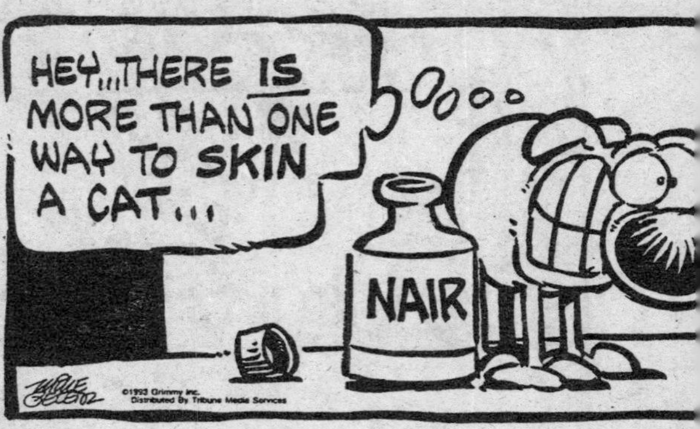
HEY...THERE IS MORE THAN ONE WAY TO SKIN A CAT...
NAIR
©1993 Grimmy Inc.
Distributed By Tribune Media Services

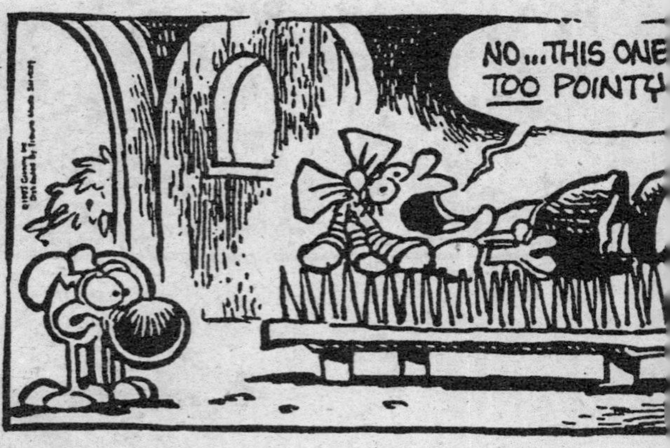
NO...THIS ONE
TOO POINTY

OLDILOCKS AND THE THREE HINDUS

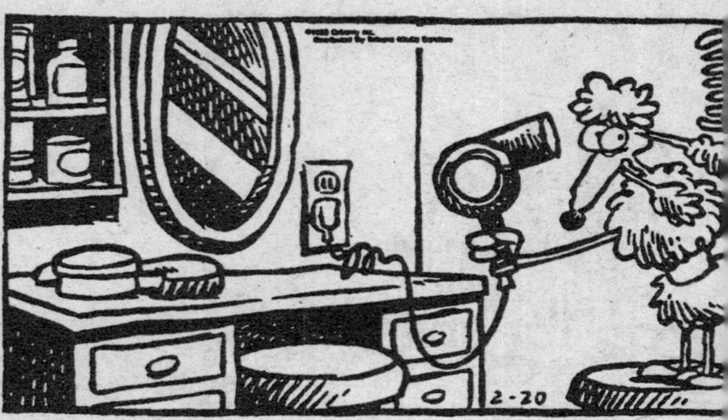
2-20

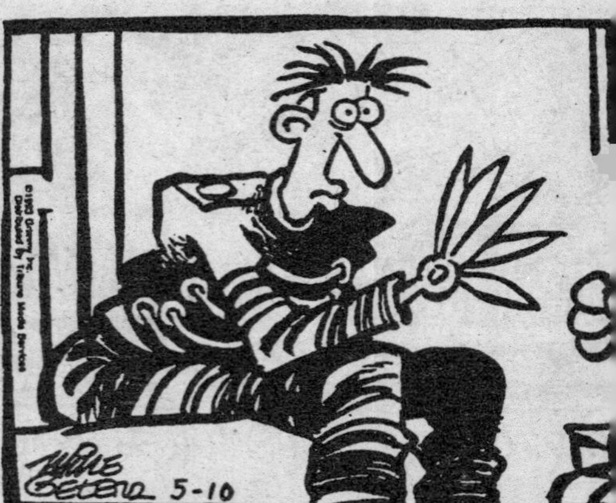
©1993 Grimm, Inc.
Distributed by Tribune Media Services
Mike Peters 5-10

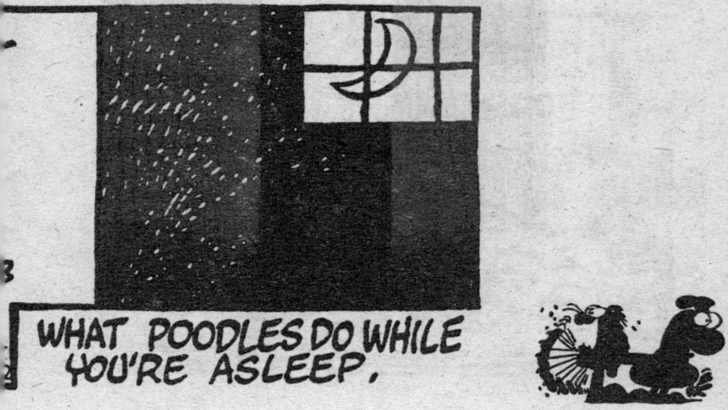
WHAT POODLES DO WHILE YOU'RE ASLEEP.

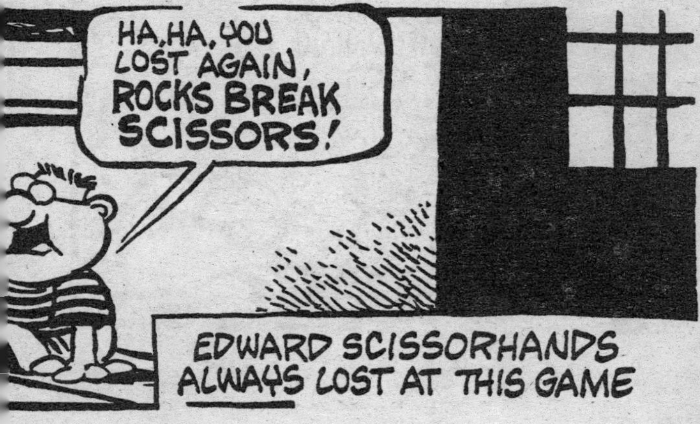
HA,HA, YOU LOST AGAIN, ROCKS BREAK SCISSORS!
EDWARD SCISSORHANDS ALWAYS LOST AT THIS GAME

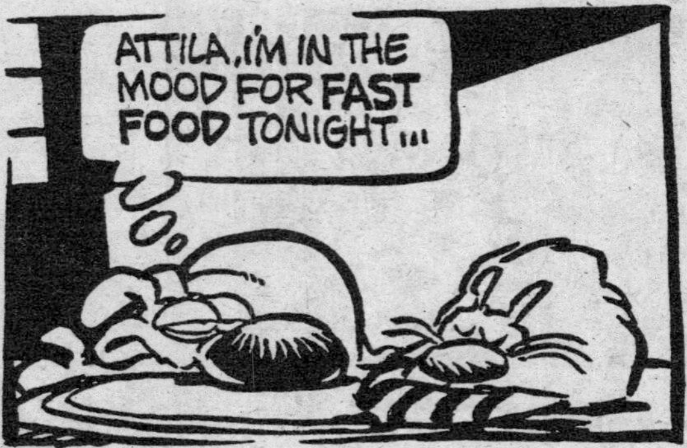
ATTILA, I'M IN THE MOOD FOR FAST FOOD TONIGHT...

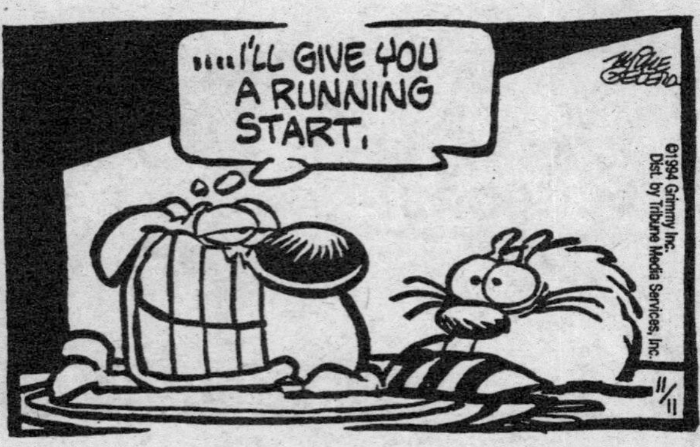
....I'LL GIVE YOU A RUNNING START.
©1994 Grimmy Inc.
Dist. by Tribune Media Services, Inc.
11/11

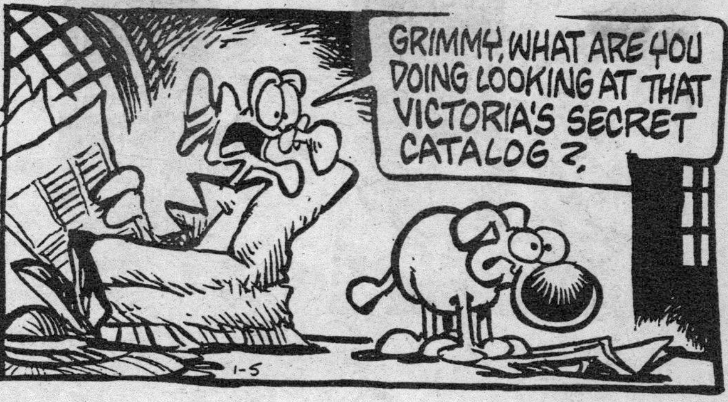
GRIMMY, WHAT ARE YOU DOING LOOKING AT THAT VICTORIA'S SECRET CATALOG?
1-5

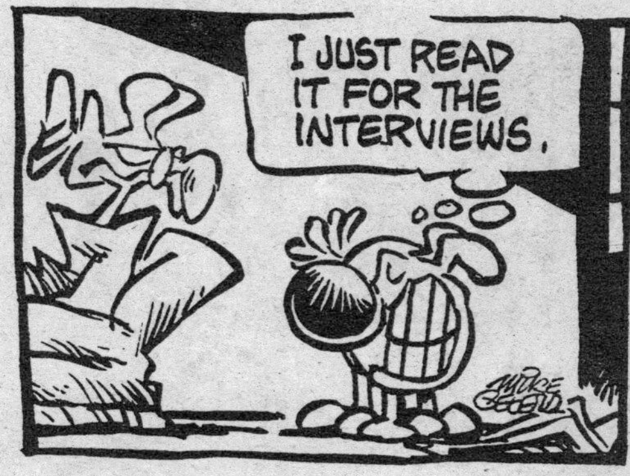
I JUST READ IT FOR THE INTERVIEWS.

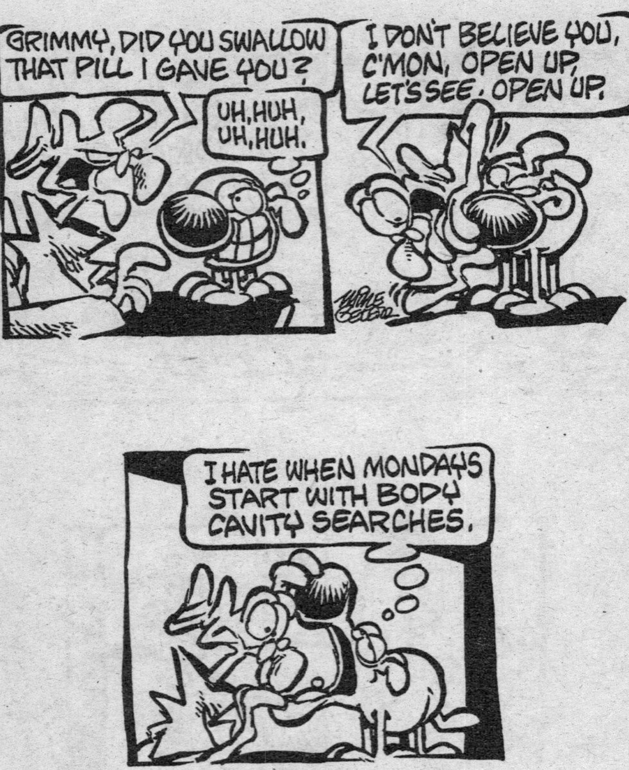
GRIMMY, DID YOU SWALLOW THAT PILL I GAVE YOU?
UH, HUH, UH, HUH.
I DON'T BELIEVE YOU, C'MON, OPEN UP, LET'S SEE. OPEN UP.
I HATE WHEN MONDAYS START WITH BODY CAVITY SEARCHES.

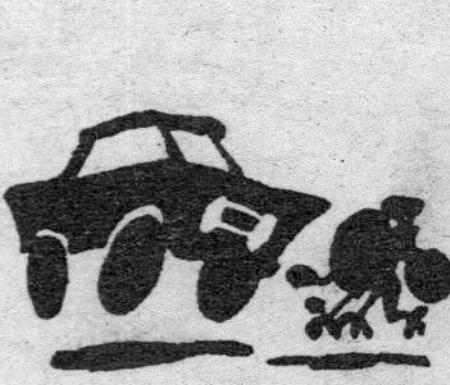

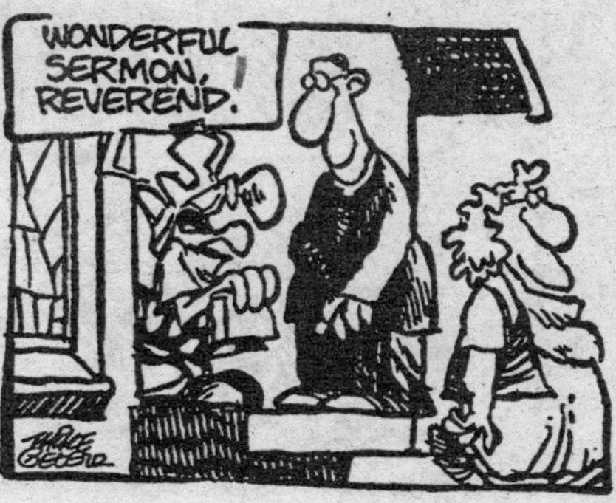
WONDERFUL SERMON, REVEREND!

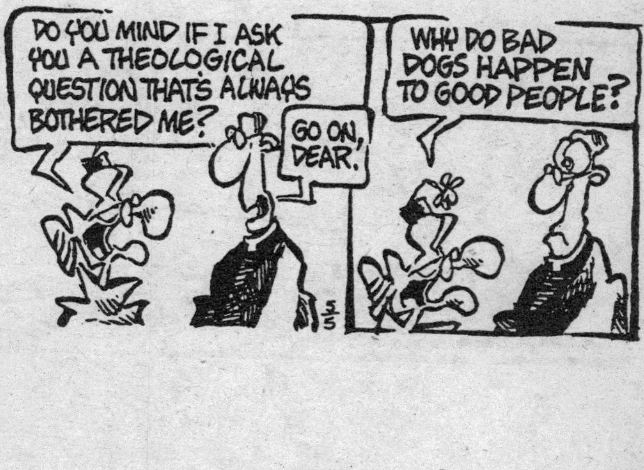
DO YOU MIND IF I ASK YOU A THEOLOGICAL QUESTION THAT'S ALWAYS BOTHERED ME?
GO ON, DEAR.
WHY DO BAD DOGS HAPPEN TO GOOD PEOPLE?

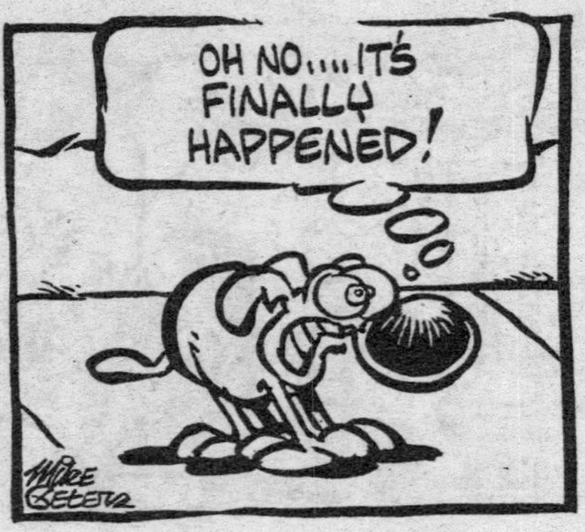
OH NO.....IT'S FINALLY HAPPENED!

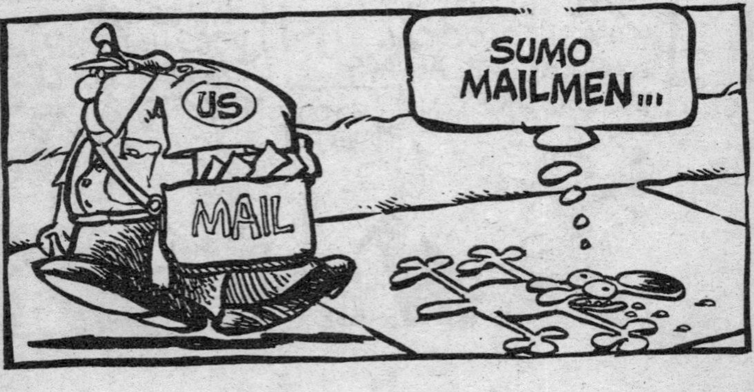
US
MAIL
SUMO MAILMEN...

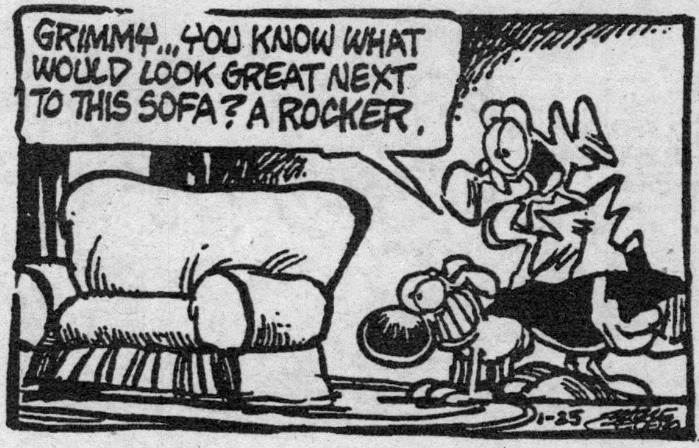
GRIMMY... YOU KNOW WHAT WOULD LOOK GREAT NEXT TO THIS SOFA? A ROCKER.
1-25

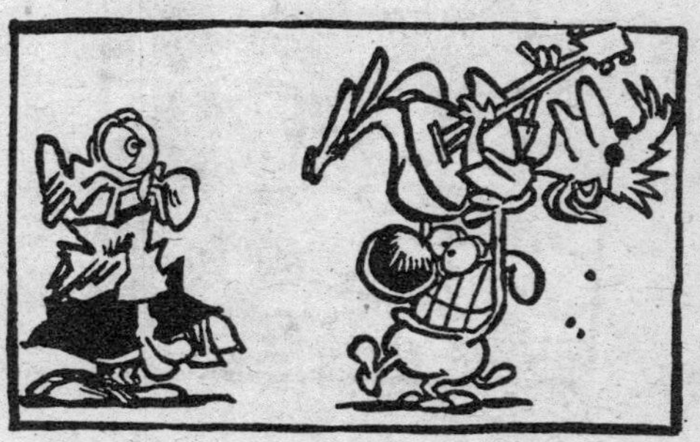

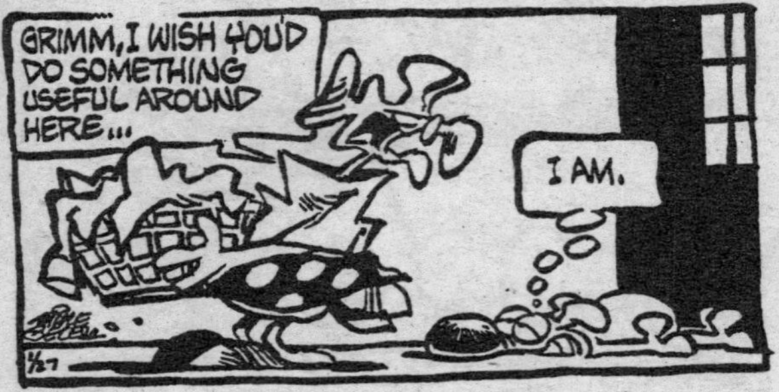
GRIMM, I WISH YOU'D DO SOMETHING USEFUL AROUND HERE...
I AM.

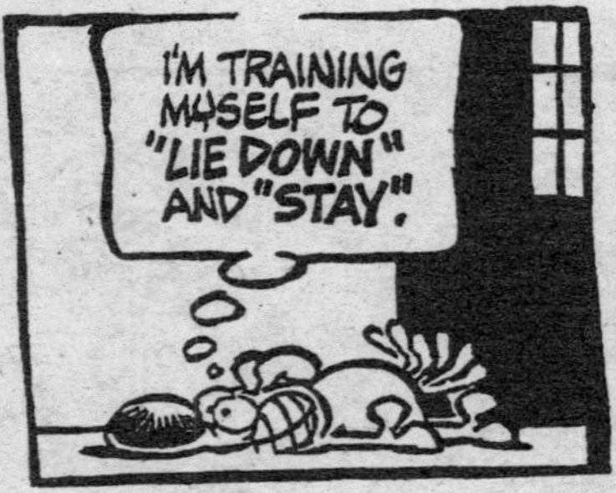
I'M TRAINING MYSELF TO "LIE DOWN" AND "STAY".

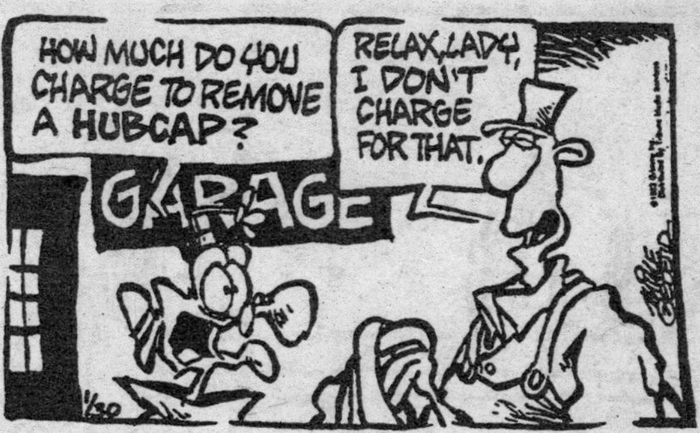
HOW MUCH DO YOU CHARGE TO REMOVE A HUBCAP?
RELAX, LADY, I DON'T CHARGE FOR THAT.
GARAGE

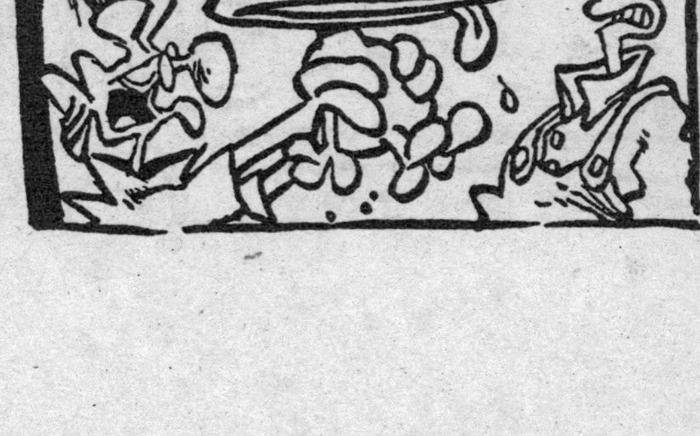
GREAT...HERE, I'LL BE BACK AT FIVE.

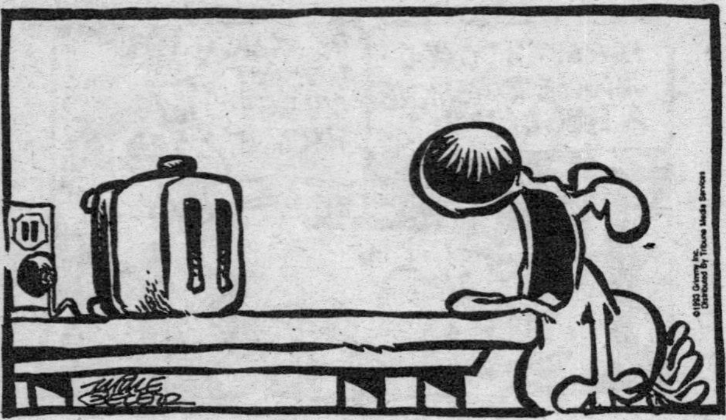
©1993 Grimmy Inc.
Distributed by Tribune Media Services

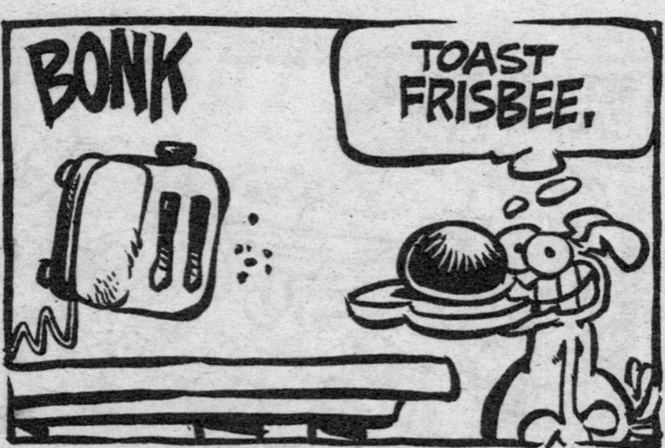
BONK
TOAST FRISBEE.

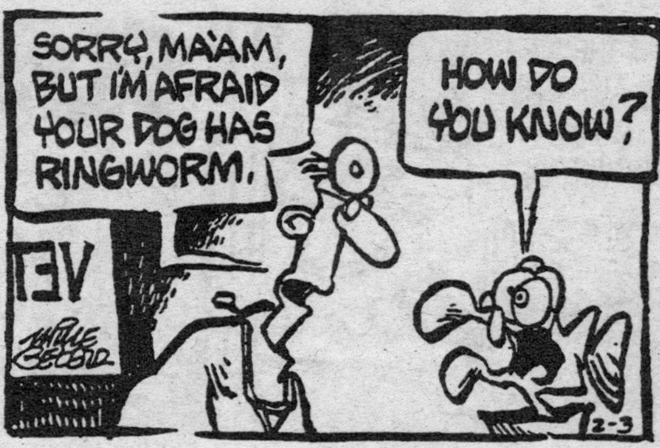
SORRY, MA'AM, BUT I'M AFRAID YOUR DOG HAS RINGWORM.
HOW DO YOU KNOW?
VET
2-3

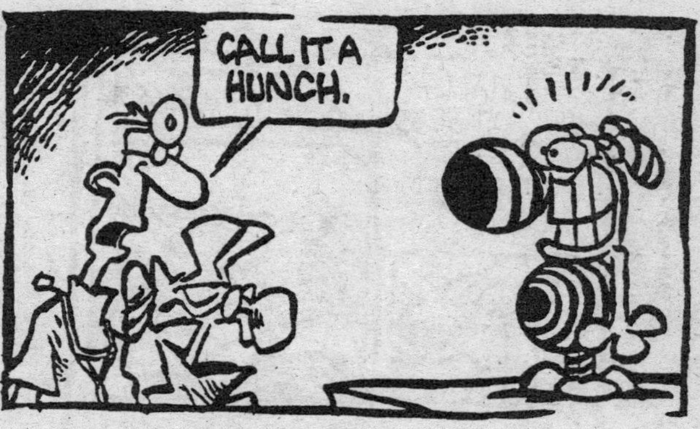
CALL IT A HUNCH.

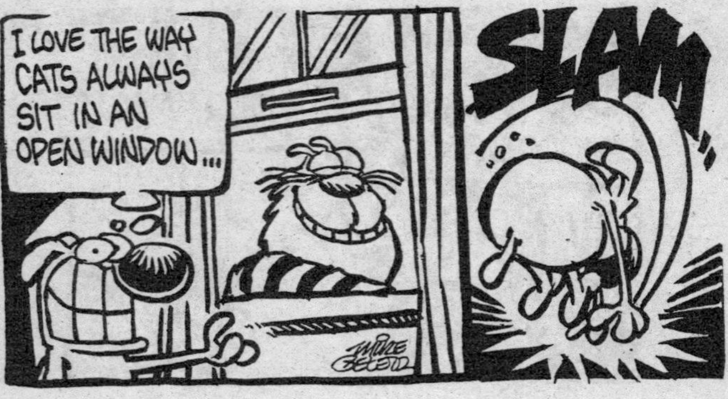
I LOVE THE WAY CATS ALWAYS SIT IN AN OPEN WINDOW...
SLAM!!
MIKE PETERS

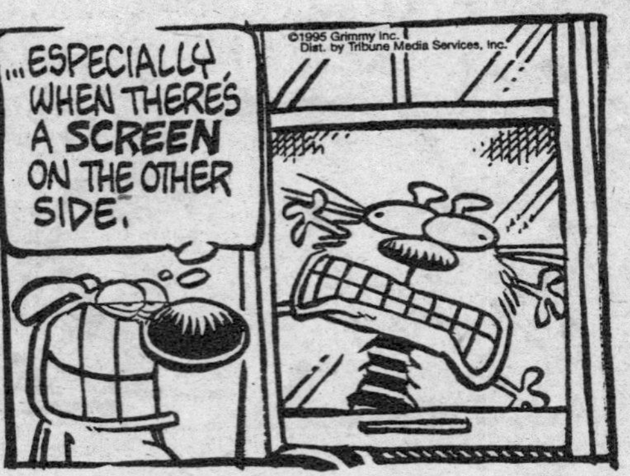
...ESPECIALLY WHEN THERE'S A SCREEN ON THE OTHER SIDE.
©1995 Grimmy Inc.
Dist. by Tribune Media Services, Inc.

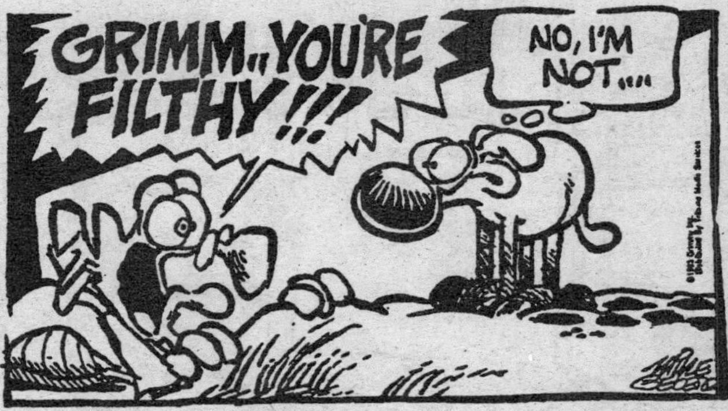
GRIMM.. YOU'RE FILTHY!!!
NO, I'M NOT....

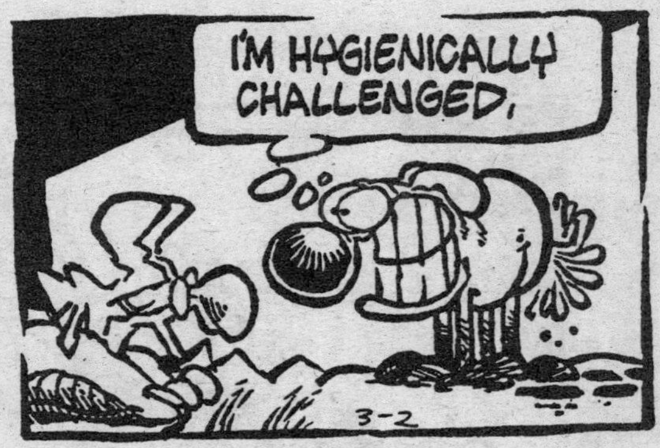
I'M HYGIENICALLY CHALLENGED.
3-2

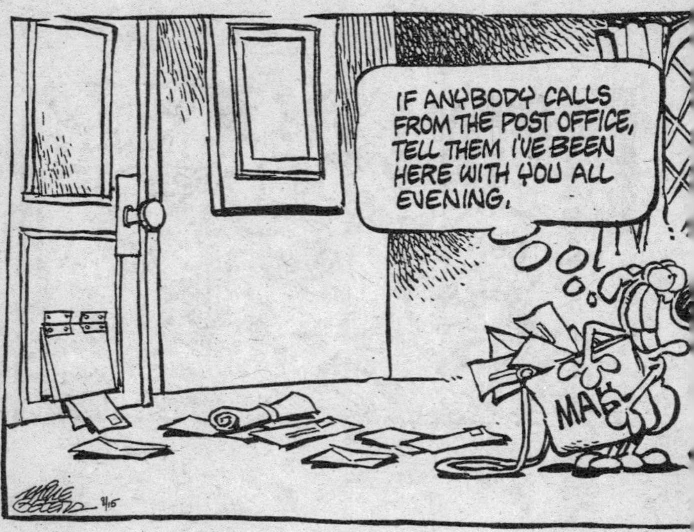
IF ANYBODY CALLS FROM THE POST OFFICE, TELL THEM I'VE BEEN HERE WITH YOU ALL EVENING.

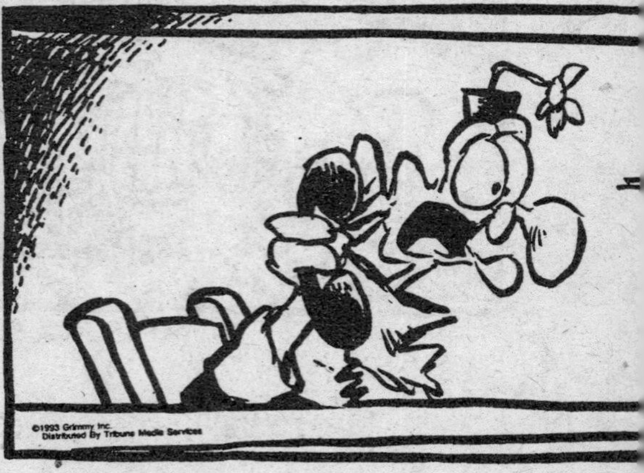
©1993 Grimmy Inc.
Distributed By Tribune Media Services

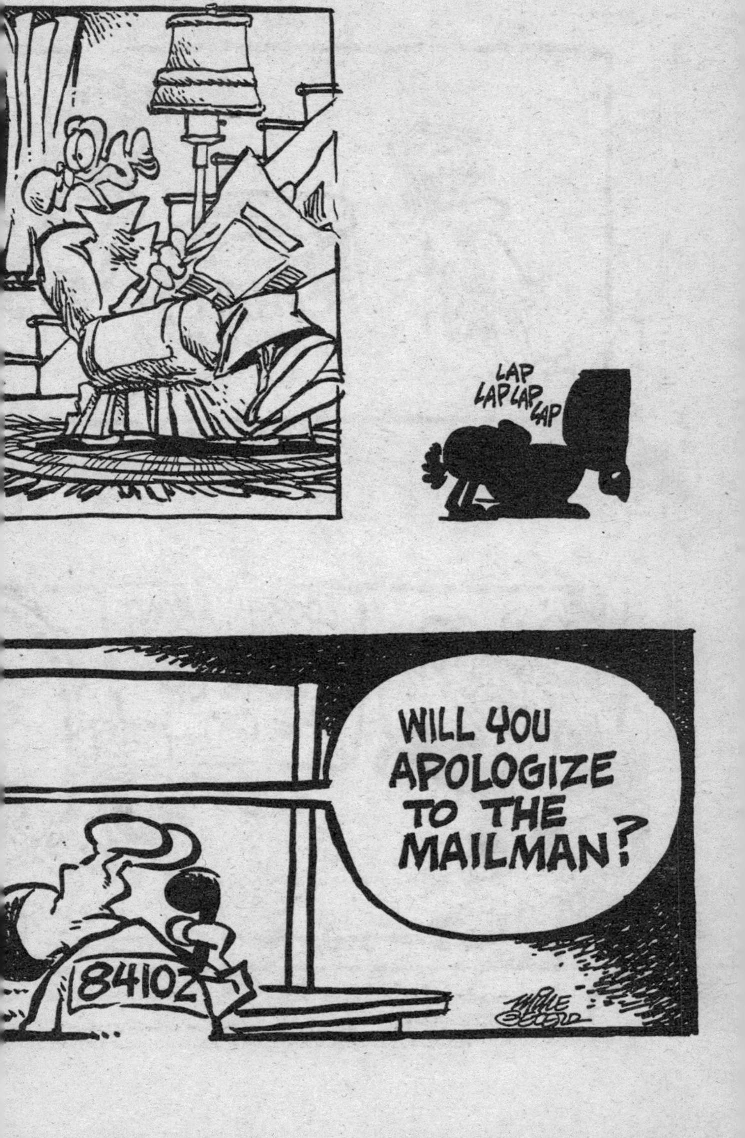
LAP
LAP LAP LAP
WILL YOU APOLOGIZE TO THE MAILMAN?
84102

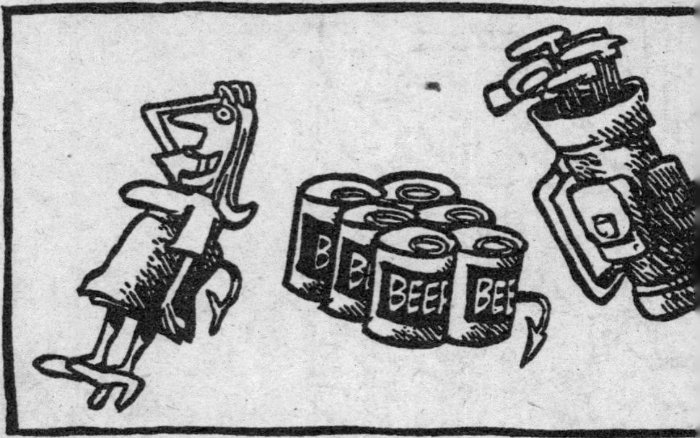

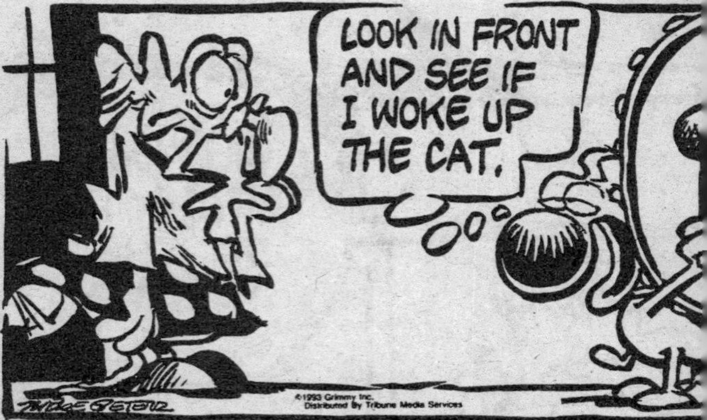
LOOK IN FRONT AND SEE IF I WOKE UP THE CAT.
©1993 Grimmy Inc.
Distributed By Tribune Media Services

GUY LURES

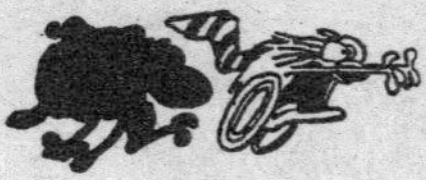

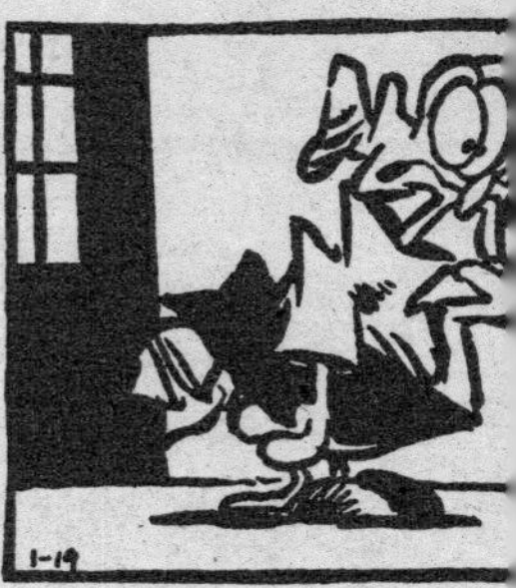
1-19

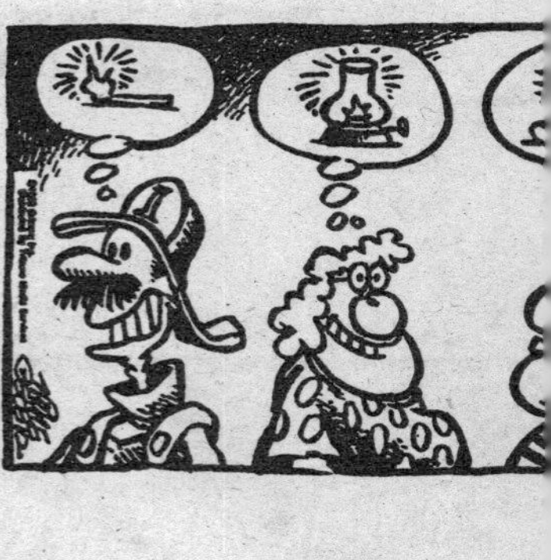

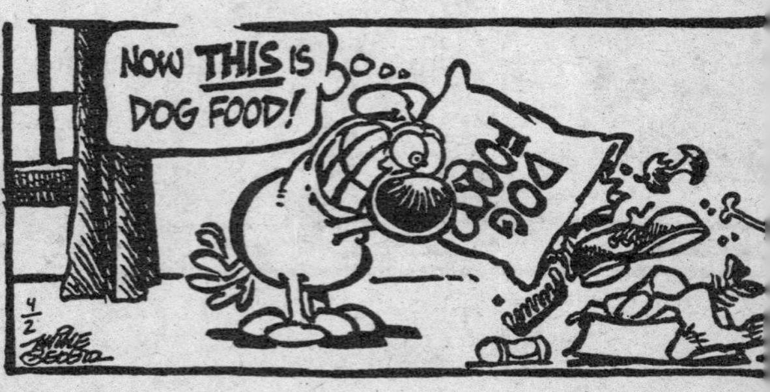
NOW THIS IS DOG FOOD!
DOG FOOD
4/2

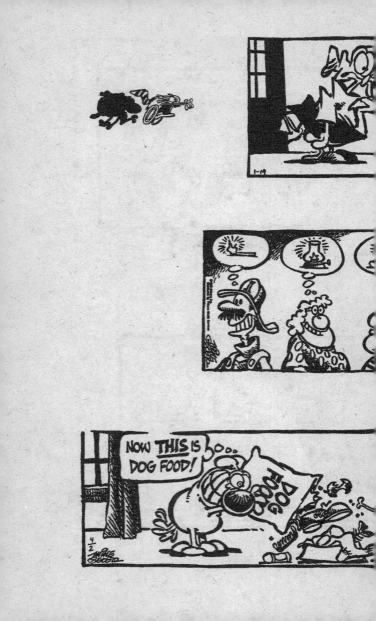

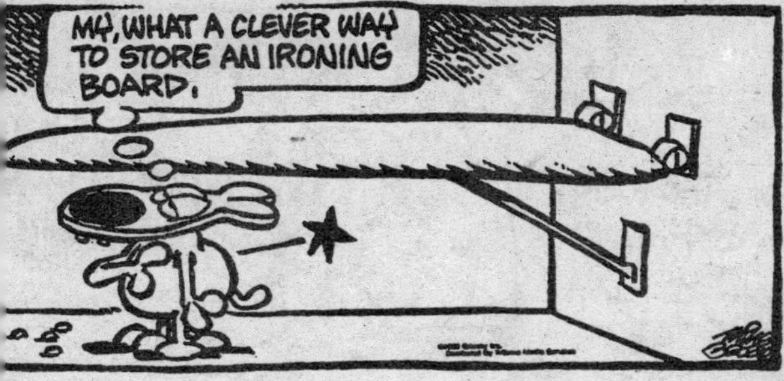
MY, WHAT A CLEVER WAY TO STORE AN IRONING BOARD.

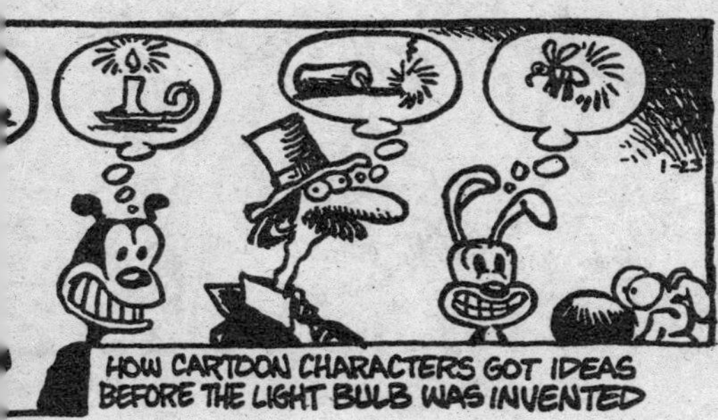
1-23

HOW CARTOON CHARACTERS GOT IDEAS BEFORE THE LIGHT BULB WAS INVENTED

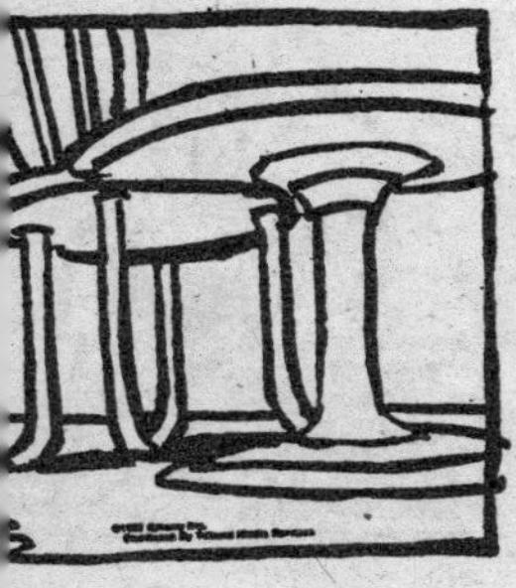

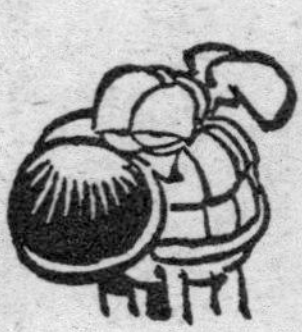

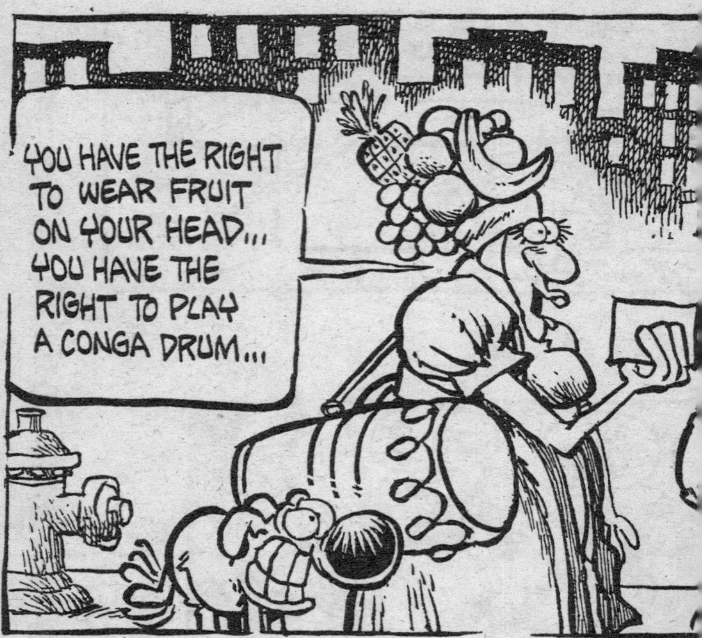
YOU HAVE THE RIGHT TO WEAR FRUIT ON YOUR HEAD... YOU HAVE THE RIGHT TO PLAY A CONGA DRUM...

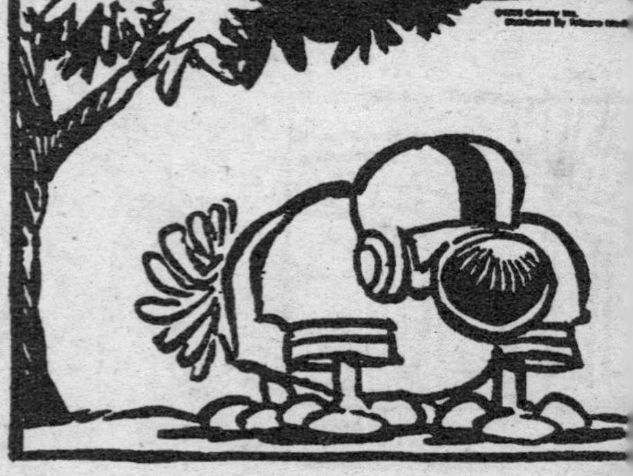

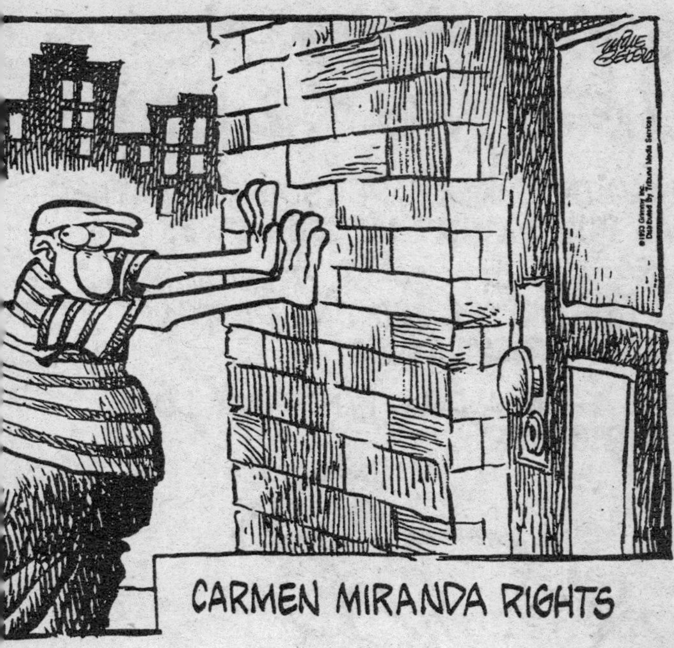
CARMEN MIRANDA RIGHTS

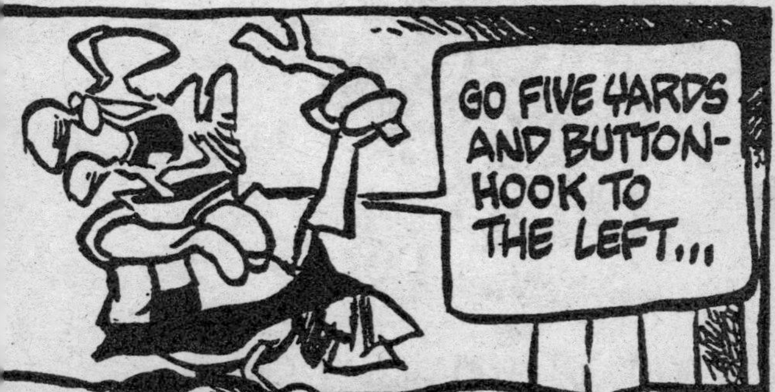
GO FIVE YARDS AND BUTTON-HOOK TO THE LEFT...

WHERE ARE THE GOODS?

MANY OF OUR READERS ASK HOW THEY CAN BUY GRIMMY MERCHANDISE.

HERE IS A LIST OF LICENSEES IN THE UNITED STATES AND CANADA THAT CARRY GREAT STUFF!

GIVE THEM A CALL FOR YOUR LOCAL DISTRIBUTOR.

WWW.GRIMMY.COM

The Antioch Company 888 Dayton St. Yellow Springs, OH 45387	PH 800/543-2397 Bookmarks, Wallet Cards, "Largely Literary" products: T-Shirts, Mugs, Journals, Pens, Notepads, Bookplates, Bookmarks
Avalanche Publishing 1093 Bedmar St. Carson, CA 90746	PH 310/223-1600 365 Day Box Calendar-Year 2000 www.avalanchepub.com
Classcom, Inc. 770 Bertrand Montreal, Quebec Canada H4M1V9	PH 514/747-9492 Desk Art
C.T.I. 22160 North Pepper Rd. Barrington, IL 60010	PH 800/284-5605 Balloons, Coffee Mugs
F.X. Schmid/USA 1 Puzzle Lane Newton, NH 03858	PH 800/886-1236 Puzzles www.fxschmid.com
Gibson Greetings 2100 Section Rd. Cincinnati, OH 45237	PH 800/345-6521 Greeting Cards, Party Papers, Gift Wrap etc... www.greetst.com
Linda Jones Enterprises 17771 Mitchell Irvine, CA 92614	PH 949/660-7791 Cels
MR. TEES 3225 Hartsfield Rd. Tallahassee, FL 32303	PH 850/574-3737 T-Shirts
Pomegranate 210 Classic Ct. Rohnert Park, CA 94928	PH 800/227-1428 Wall Year 2000 Calendars, Postcard Booklets www.pomegranate.com
Second Nature Software 1325 Officers' Row Vancouver, WA 98661	PH 360/737-4170 Screen Saver Program www.secondnature.com
TOR Books 175 Fifth Ave. New York, NY 10010	PH 212/388-0100 Paperback Books www.tor.com
Western Graphics 3535 W. 1st Avenue Eugene, OR 97402	PH 800/532-3303 Posters